THE INCLUSIVE TEAM

How to Build and Develop Inclusive High Performing Teams

Melody Moore

authors
AND CO.

CONTENTS

This book is dedicated to my daughter Holly. I hope that by the time you are my age many of the topics in this book will seem like ancient history.

I also dedicate this book to my dad, who has dementia and doesn't know I've written a book but would be so incredibly proud if he did.

INTRODUCTION

"If you want to go fast, go alone. If you want to go far, go together."

— *AFRICAN PROVERB*

WHO IS THIS BOOK FOR?

This book is for you if you want a practical guide to building a genuinely inclusive and high performing team.

You might be a DEI professional, a team leader/member, a senior leader, or a Learning & Development consultant. Maybe you are an expert and have tried various approaches to building inclusion, or maybe you are at the beginning of your journey. Whatever the case, this book is for you if you recognise the power of engaging team members to collectively create an inclusive and high performing environment.

You can use this book purely with your own team or as a framework for working with many different teams to create a new and different approach to building an inclusive and high performing organisation.

It is designed to be practical – you can take what you read and apply it immediately. It will help you understand the building blocks of an inclusive high performing team and will give you plenty of practical tips and exercises to explore what it means in practice for your team.

This book is based on the Liberare Consulting The Inclusive Team™ model which I, Melody Moore, have developed based on my twenty plus years as a consultant to hundreds of UK and global organisations. I am a psychologist, consultant and coach and have many years of experience helping leaders, teams and organisations improve their performance.

You may notice that while the title is *The Inclusive Team*, the subtitle references a high performing team. This is because DEI shouldn't be a stand-alone topic or approach – it should be integrated into the everyday fabric of an organisation. We need to ensure that the inclusive teams we create are also high performing. Whilst there is an overlap between the two, they are not the same thing.

This model brings elements of Diversity, Inclusion and High Performing Teams into one integrated approach, and I believe it is the first team model that does so. However, 'The Diverse and Inclusive and High Performing Team model' was a bit of a mouthful! I opted for *The Inclusive Team* to differentiate it from other models of team effectiveness.

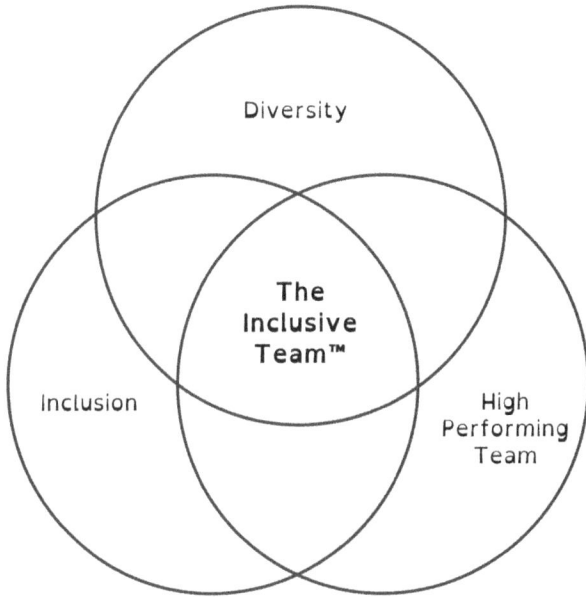

How to Read this Book

In my view, most business books are too long, and often repeat the same ideas over and over. My aim was to keep this book reasonably short and very practical. The introduction covers some background concepts around teams and DEI; thereafter the book is divided into two parts.

The five chapters of Part One each cover a cluster from The Inclusive Team™ model and introduce the behaviours in each cluster, alongside tips for leaders and team members, plus exercises to help teams develop the cluster.

In Part Two, the focus turns to your application and implementation of The Inclusive Team™ approach. I describe several delivery options and how you might tackle some of the challenges and resistance you may face.

This isn't a review of the academic literature, so it won't be written in that style, but I have included a list of resources at the end of each chapter for those of you who want to dig a little deeper.

Accompanying materials for the exercises can be downloaded via the Liberare Consulting website. This includes a ten-question survey you can use with your team to identify strengths and areas for development. Find your link to access these resources at the back of the book.

You don't have to read the book from cover to cover. You might want to focus on particular chapters that interest you. I recommend reading the introduction to cover some fundamentals, but after that – follow your heart!

Why Is DEI Important?

There are many books and articles already written that highlight the importance of DEI for organisations, so my intention is not to try to convince you that you should be trying to create a more diverse and inclusive workplace. You would not have started this book if you weren't already a little convinced! You may, however, not be particularly experienced in DEI so it may be helpful to cover a few basic principles.

Terminology

Language and terminology are complex topics, and I cover them in more detail in the Respect chapter. Below are my definitions of some of the key terms I will be using throughout the book.

Diversity: This is about valuing the full range of human differences and similarities, including the intersectionality of our differences. When we talk about diverse teams or organisations, we mean ensuring that a broad range of people with different demographics are represented in the team or throughout the organisation (including at the top). You can learn more about this in the Respect chapter.

Equity: This is different from equality, which is about treating everyone the same. Equity is about ensuring that everyone has the same access to opportunities – recognising that we start in different places and that sometimes, in order to be fair, we may need to treat people differently, for example, development programmes for specific under-represented groups. The image below summarises the difference nicely.

In the image on the left everyone is being treated equally: they all have the same size box. In the picture on the right, their differences are recognised, and they have different boxes that allow all of them to see over the fence – this is equity.

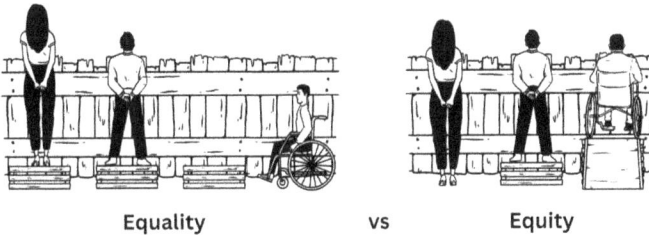

Equality   vs   Equity

Inclusion: This is about the behaviours and processes that ensure people feel valued and included, and that a range of perspectives are heard. If Diversity is being asked to the party, then Inclusion is being asked to dance! There is no point creating a more diverse organisation if you don't also have an inclusive culture. It will lead to conflict, disappointment and high turnover.

Under-represented group: This is any group of people who share a particular demographic who are under-represented in the workplace. To know if a group is under-represented, we often compare the percentage representation in the organisation with the percentage representation in the population. For example, in the 2021 UK Census, we can see that 17.8 percent of the UK population is disabled. However, the populations of many of the organisations I work with include a disabled population of less than ten percent.

Please note that I prefer this term to *minority group.* Some groups (e.g. women) are not in the minority but are still under-represented at certain levels in the workplace.

High performing team: What high performance looks like will be different depending on your context, but I mean a team that consistently outperforms its peers. It is not a DEI term, but I will use it throughout the book.

To help you take a broader look at the DEI landscape, I have included a couple of suggestions in the references which conclude this chapter. You will also find a link to a DEI glossary from Diverse Educators, and in the Respect chapter you can read further discussion on the importance of inclusive language.

Business Case

We often hear talk of the business case for DEI. You may be uncomfortable with needing to make a business case for something that feels to you like a moral imperative, but my experience tells me it is actually a very important part of creating a more diverse, equitable and inclusive culture. In my mind, the moral case is part of the overall business case. Changing behaviours and culture is hard work, and we must be able to understand and articulate why we are doing it in a way that grabs the hearts *and* minds of our colleagues.

We will cover this in more depth in Part Two, where we talk about team and organisational implementation, but for now, let's understand that organisations tend to focus on DEI for three main reasons:

1. **Compliance** – they don't want to break the law, or they have to report their diversity data, or there are government mandated quotas.

Compliance with Law: For instance, organisations in the UK are governed by the Equality Act 2010 which protects employees and consumers (and potential employees such as job applicants) from unfair treatment in areas such as recruitment, working practices, pay and benefits, promotion, etc. The act covers nine 'protected characteristics' (age, gender reassignment, being married or in a civil partnership, being pregnant or on maternity leave, disability, race, religion or belief, sex, sexual orientation).

Outside the UK, each country (and in some cases each state/region within a country) has its own laws. The groups which are protected and the levels of protection they are offered vary widely.

Compliance with reporting: In the UK, organisations of over two hundred and fifty employees must publicly report on their gender pay gap. In the USA, companies with over one hundred employees must disclose the gender and ethnicity of employees to the US Equal Employment Opportunity Commission (but public disclosure is voluntary).

Compliance with quotas: Some countries have taken things a step further and introduced quotas. For example, some countries in Europe have laws mandating quotas. In France a law was introduced in 2021 stating that thirty percent of all boardroom positions should be held by women by 2027 rising to forty percent by

2030. This applies to all companies with at least one thousand employees. Other countries have 'soft' quotas that are not mandated by law. For example, Denmark's corporate governance recommendations oblige listed companies to set up goals for gender equality on their boards.

2. Values – they believe it's the right thing to do.

Often referred to as the moral business case, this is based on the principles of fairness and equal opportunity for all.

3. Business – they do it because it makes good business sense.

There are two elements to this. Firstly, there is an increasing body of research showing that increasing diversity and developing inclusive practices have a positive impact on an organisation's performance and bottom line. Organisations that are more diverse and inclusive can access the 'diversity dividend'.

- Female directors on a company board correlated with a decreased risk of declaring bankruptcy. (Wilson, 2009)
- Women in senior leadership roles improved board and organisational financial performance, innovation and decision making. (Bourne et al 2016, Nolan & Moran, 2016)
- McKinsey found that companies in the top quartile for ethnic and cultural diversity in their top team outperformed those in the fourth quartile by thirty-six percent in terms of profitability (McKinsey, Diversity Wins, 2019)
- A study of 7,600 firms in London found that companies with diverse top teams are more likely than those with

homogeneous top management to introduce new product innovations. (Nathan & Lee, 2013)

The second element of DEI making good business sense comprises a range of other business reasons.

- Customer, employee and shareholder expectations/demands.
- Other external pressures such as government reviews (e.g. the Hampton-Alexander review that looked at the number of women on UK FTSE Boards).
- A company's desire to reflect their customers' demographics in their workforce.
- To attract and retain top talent.

People often talk of 'the business case for DEI' as though it is a single unilateral thing. This is not the case; therefore, when building an inclusive team, it is important that you understand and clearly articulate why DEI is important to you as an individual, and to work collectively to identify the business case for you as a team.

Some people take a somewhat reductive approach and try to argue that some reasons are better or more important than others. It is natural that each organisation, team and individual will have their own reasons and they are likely to combine elements from all three categories. Thus, when I talk about 'the business case for DEI' I include within that description the potential for a combination of compliance, values and business reasons.

SOME THOUGHTS ON TEAMS

Team Versus Work Group

There is a difference between a team and a work group. In a team, the members work together to achieve a shared aim or common goal – they have mutual accountability. In a work group, members may coordinate their efforts, but tend to work more independently and have individual accountability.

A good question to ask is: *What can we achieve collectively that we can't individually?* If the answer is 'nothing', you are likely to be a work group rather than a team.

Work Group vs Team

Work Group		Team
Same as organisation	Objectives/Purpose	Specific to team
Individual	Goals/ Accountability	Individual and Shared
Share information and perspectives. Work is divided up.	Type of Work	Discuss, decide, problem solving, work is done together
Independent	Dependencies	Interdependent

The Inclusive Team™ model is designed to capture the behaviours and mindsets that make a high performing, inclusive team. Some of its elements will help a work group be more effective, but the focus is mainly on team behaviours.

Why Do We Have Teams?

Before we dive into the details of an inclusive team, we should understand why teams exist in the first place, and how they feed into our normal ways of living and working.

Biological Drive

The formation of teams or groups is a natural state for human beings. Even those of us who think of ourselves as independent souls who don't need others are biologically programmed to connect and be part of groups. We are born physically premature; we are unable to fend for ourselves for many years and therefore are highly dependent on our caretakers. This means we are pre-programmed to make social connections – to seek to engage others – as our survival as children depends on it.

Research shows that being in groups has a positive effect on our health even as adults. Fewer social ties are associated with an increased likelihood of heart disease, cancer, and impaired immune function, as well as with worse recovery when it comes to these health problems. Other research suggests that people with weaker social networks are likely to die younger.

As mammals, we live in a constant state of alertness to threat, and when we perceive threat, our nervous systems are triggered. Nowadays a threat is less likely to be, *Will this wild animal eat me?* We are more triggered by social threats to things that are important to us such as status, relationships or fairness. The nervous system responds to everything we experience, and we move between feelings of safety and threat all the time. As consultant and neuroscience expert Hilary Scarlett puts it, 'Our brains are not designed to see the world as it is, but in a way that keeps us safe... Our brains tend to discount the positives and amplify the negatives because the latter are more significant in terms of safety and survival.'

Threat is experienced in the part of our brain called the limbic system, which reacts far more quickly than the prefrontal cortex (where our cognitive skills, creativity, speech and language processing take place). Thus, when our perception of threat is too high, more oxygen goes to the limbic system and our ability to access the prefrontal cortex is compromised. We are all familiar with the concept of fight, flight or freeze: this is what happens when we perceive a threat in the workplace.

I am sure you can think of a time when your fight, flight or freeze mechanism kicked in at work and you were unable to think or be at your best. It might have been a particular senior manager who was impatient, and you found yourself frozen and unable to answer their rapid-fire questions, even though you knew the answers. Or perhaps you had to speak in front of hundreds of colleagues at a conference and you found your palms sweating, your heart racing, and you stuttered over your words despite having been word perfect when you practised at home.

There are two key ways to regulate your nervous system – self-regulation, where you learn to soothe yourself and reduce your nervous system's response to threat, and co-regulation, where you rely on someone else to help you regulate your nervous system.

The very presence of another person you trust can have a positive impact on your nervous system, and even on how you perceive things. An interesting study by Simone Schnall and colleagues in 2008 found that people estimated a hill was less steep when they were accompanied by a friend than when they were alone. In fact, just thinking of a supportive friend helped the study participants perceive the hill as less steep. The friend didn't even have to be physically present to have a positive effect.

This research really resonates with me. When I was a novice snowboarder, I thought the nursery slopes looked like the north face of the Eiger. A few weeks later the exact same slopes looked as flat as the salt flats in Utah! I was amazed by the alteration in my perception.

There is significant potential for our nervous system to be over-stimulated by the workplace, which has a negative effect on our performance. The Inclusive Team™ framework will help you build a safe, supportive and challenging team environment where you can practise co-regulation and ensure that the nervous systems of your people experience just the right amount of threat to help them perform at their best, but not so much threat that they feel overwhelmed and their performance suffers – see the Growth chapter for more on creating this zone of optimal performance.

Collective Intelligence

In addition to biological, physiological reasons, teams exist for many practical, business focused reasons. One answer lies in Aristotle's suggestion that 'the whole is greater than the sum of its parts.' There is potentially a collective intelligence in a team exponentially greater than the intelligence of individual members.

However, there is an interesting twist to this. As Roderick Swaab and his team from INSEAD identify, there is not a linear relationship between the amount of talent on a team and performance. We can all think of sports teams that are full of incredible individual players but fail to live up to their combined potential. (Hello, England men's football team!)

Anita Williams Woolley researches the concept of collective intelligence. She states: 'The groups with the greatest collective intelligence are not those with the smartest person or even the smartest group of people, but groups who have the capacity to solve problems through social coordination.' This is similar to (but slightly different from) what some people refer to as the 'hive mind' – which is a group of people to whom we can reach out who will readily share our knowledge and opinions. Collective intelligence takes this one step further and is about collaborative problem solving and development of new ideas.

The research suggests that certain key behaviours enable a group of talented people to reach their collective potential, and if those key behaviours are missing the team will not be high performing, even if it is made up of brilliant individuals. The most significant indicator of the collective intelligence of the team is how well they collaborate and coordinate. Take a look at the Alignment chapter if you want to know more about this.

Teams in the Modern World

A high performing team is one that consistently performs well in comparison to their peers. There are many models of high performing teams. However, they do not usually explicitly call out the importance of team diversity and inclusive behaviours. This is an oversight: inclusive behaviours are an essential element to help teams cope with the complexity of our modern world.

We live in what is often described as a VUCA or BANI world. The acronym VUCA evolved in the 1980s and stands for Volatile, Uncertain, Complex and Ambiguous. More recently some organisations have started using the acronym BANI, which stands for Brittle, Anxious, Non-linear and Incomprehensible. There are some differences and similarities between the two, but both attempt to describe the chaotic world in which we live. I'm a bit old school so prefer VUCA and will use that throughout this book, but know that when I say VUCA I also mean BANI. Check out the references if you are interested in exploring the two further.

Regardless of the acronym we use, all organisations are affected by global trends or megatrends that impact our world. These large, ongoing trends shape our world and have an impact on how we live and work. If you Google 'global megatrends' you will find various reports, lists and articles each with a slightly different way of clustering the trends. The graphic below shows what I believe to be the five main ones. Take a look and identify which trends affect your organisation right now.

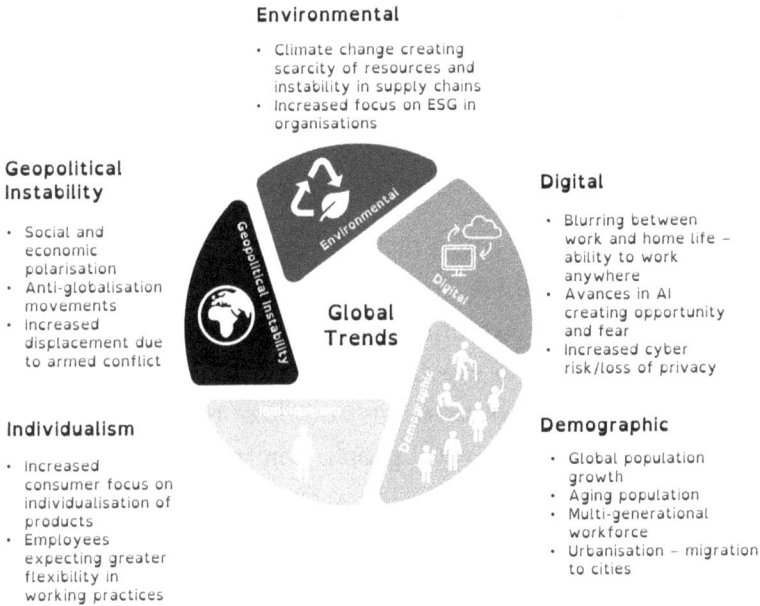

Environmental
- Climate change creating scarcity of resources and instability in supply chains
- Increased focus on ESG in organisations

Geopolitical Instability
- Social and economic polarisation
- Anti-globalisation movements
- Increased displacement due to armed conflict

Global Trends

Digital
- Blurring between work and home life – ability to work anywhere
- Avances in AI creating opportunity and fear
- Increased cyber risk/loss of privacy

Individualism
- Increased consumer focus on individualisation of products
- Employees expecting greater flexibility in working practices

Demographic
- Global population growth
- Aging population
- Multi-generational workforce
- Urbanisation – migration to cities

In order for organisations to thrive in the VUCA world where global megatrends create instability and opportunity, they need to be flexible and innovative, able to react to rapid changes in circumstances.

We have all heard of Blockbuster, Blackberry, Yahoo, Kodak and Nokia. At one time these organisations were all at the top of their game – world famous, sector leading brands that seemed invincible. They all, however, have fallen from grace; some have collapsed completely, while others are a shadow of their former selves. One thing they have in common is that they failed to spot the external trends that indicated they needed to change the way they did business. They all failed to be flexible, and they failed to innovate.

One of the reasons organisations struggle to accept that the world around them is changing is that of 'groupthink'. This is a strong urge to conform to a dominant way of thinking. People feel like they can't disagree, and conflict must be avoided. It is more common when people have similar ways of thinking, and where there are strong group norms favouring agreement over conflict. There are many famous examples of groupthink, including the Challenger space shuttle disaster and the demise of SwissAir.

Reviews of the circumstances that led to the collapse of the organisations mentioned above tend to cite a degree of groupthink, often caused by the recruitment of people with similar backgrounds, education and experience who fail to grasp the seriousness of their situation because it is outside of their experience. If we surround ourselves with people similar to us, and only consume information from a narrow range of places, we operate in an echo chamber where we think we hear a range of opinions but in truth we just hear a version of our own views reflected back at us.

Whilst your team or organisation might not face such fundamental threats to your existence, it is still essential that you can adapt and innovate in order to react to the constant changes in the environment that we all experience (Covid 19 anyone?), or to ensure that the products and services we design are suitable for all. As Charles Darwin once said, 'It is not the strongest of the species that survives, nor the most intelligent, but the one most responsive to change.' This is discussed in more depth in the Adaptability chapter.

Modern teams are frequently transient, dispersed, matrixed, virtual, temporary and global, and if they are to perform well it is essential we pay close attention not just to what the team is doing, but to how it operates. This model gives you a framework to do just that – and we explore a focus on team development in more detail in the Growth chapter.

Matrixed Teams

There is sometimes confusion as to whether a team in a matrixed structure can be a real team, and my simple answer is 'yes'. Teams do not have to have formal line management relationships inside them. Some of the most successful high performing teams I have seen are project teams that have come together from across the business for a short period of time to achieve a clear and specific aim.

As you explore The Inclusive Team™ model, you will see very little mention of formal line management relationships. The philosophy of the model is that building a team is not the sole responsibility of the leader – team members share accountability for creating an inclusive and high performing team, thus the importance of the hierarchical structure is reduced.

In fact, focusing on the behaviours in the model will help reduce some of the challenges faced by individuals who work in a matrixed structure because it can help create clarity. The key is that the team members identify with the team purpose, feel they are part of the team and feel accountable for its success. They can do this whilst also being part of another team or work group. There is no rule that says you can't successfully be part of more than one team.

Virtual Teams

Since the Covid-19 pandemic, which created a huge shift to remote working, there has been a lot of discussion about virtual and hybrid working teams. This isn't the forum to get into a discussion of the pros and cons of different working patterns, but we do know that virtual and hybrid teams need higher levels of trust than teams who work in the same office day to day.

If you work in a virtual or hybrid way, you need to give extra attention to the behaviours outlined in this book that drive high performance in your team. You need to intentionally create opportunities for certain things to happen that would occur naturally if the team were all based in the same office.

These could include:

- Providing technology to enable easy communication and tracking of shared projects.
- Building in team additional bonding and relationship building time – face to face as well as virtual since the natural social opportunities that occur from working in the same place each day do not exist.
- Working particularly hard to provide clarity.
- Paying close attention to who is more (and less) visible and ensuring you don't succumb to proximity bias (where you favour people simply because they are around you more often). This is particularly true of hybrid working teams if some team members are in the office more than others.

THE INCLUSIVE TEAM

The Inclusive Team™ model was developed after working for over twenty years with leaders and teams across a range of sectors, organisations, geographies and hierarchical levels. Having led the UK and Ireland DEI practice for a global consultancy, I was frustrated with the fact that everyone focused on creating inclusive leaders (Inclusive Leadership training) and inclusive individuals (Unconscious Bias/Conscious Inclusion training), but nobody recognised that inclusion mostly takes place, and has the most impact, at a team level.

Research by *Training* magazine and The Ken Blanchard Companies found that people spend more than half of their work time in teams. It therefore seemed like a no brainer to focus my attention on creating inclusive teams, and to highlight that everyone in the team shares responsibility for creating an inclusive team environment, not just the leader.

I shared some research previously that shows the benefits of DEI at an organisational level. There is also research that shows that diverse teams outperform homogenous teams. For example:

- Research on R&D teams in Spain found that gender diversity was positively related to radical innovation. (Díaz-García et al., 2013)
- Teams with a mix of women and men outperformed all-male teams (Bear & Woolley, 2011)

However, working in diverse teams is harder than in homogenous teams – it requires more effort from all concerned and it may feel less fluid or fluent to work in a diverse team. We typically have a bias that means we trust something more easily if it is easy to process (this is known as the fluency heuristic).

Thus, we think that homogeneous teams are more effective because there is typically a fluency and ease in the way we work together. However, research suggests the opposite is true – that the conflict and challenge that come with working in a diverse team actually create a better outcome and mean we are much less likely to succumb to groupthink.

This is a challenge for organisations because they tend to gloss over or not recognise the challenges that diversity brings. By recognising both the challenges and the benefits, organisations can ensure that they support diverse teams to be as effective and high performing as possible. This means focusing not just on the diversity of the team, but the inclusive behaviours too.

It was important to me to create a model that didn't just focus on diversity and inclusivity, as my work with teams has shown me that other aspects of team performance are also highly important, and that inclusion alone isn't the answer. Behnam Tabrizi studied ninety-five cross-functional teams in twenty-five leading corporations and found that nearly 75 percent of these teams were dysfunctional. The *Training* magazine research mentioned above found that 43 percent of respondents said their teams operate at optimum levels less than fifty percent of the time. A study by Korn Ferry and Harvard of the effectiveness of 120 executive teams found that an incredible 79 percent were rated as mediocre or poor. It is clear that teams need help to be high performing as well as inclusive; hence The Inclusive Team™ model was born.

The Inclusive Team™ Model

The framework has been developed through my experience of working with existing teams models and combining it with key elements of my DEI knowledge, some aspects of neuroscience, and inspiration from concepts such as Growth Mindset (Carol Dweck), Psychological Safety (Amy Edmondson) and Intellectual Humility (Shane Snow). See the reference section if you'd like to dig deeper into any of these. The result is five clusters – Trust, Alignment, Growth, Adaptability and Respect – and ten sub-clusters (shown on the outside of the model) that capture the key elements of an inclusive high performing team as illustrated in the diagram below.

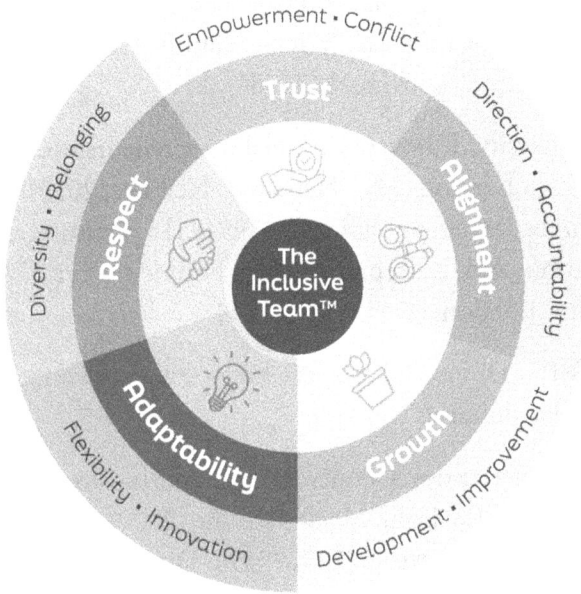

The clusters are both distinct and inter-related. For instance, some elements of the Innovation sub-cluster are unique to that cluster, but they will be greatly enhanced if the team also has high levels of Trust.

WHAT NEXT?

Now that you have been introduced to some of the key topics and terminology, take a look at the contents page and dive into one of the chapters that interests you most.

REFERENCES

BANI - How to Make Sense of a Chaotic World? - https://thinkin sights.net/leadership/bani/

Brainpower at Work (Hilary Scarlett) - https://amzn.to/49rCJiw

Billion Dollar Lessons: What you Can Learn from the Inexcusable Business Failures of the Last 25 Years (Paul B Carroll and Chunka Mui, 2008) - https://amzn.to/462578Q

Cultural Diversity, Innovation, and Entrepreneurship: Firm-level Evidence from London (Max Nathan & Neil Lee, 2013) - https://www.researchgate.net/publication/259548515_Cultural_Diversity_Innovation_and_Entrepreneurship_Firm-level_Evidence_from_London

DEI Glossary - Diverse Educators - https://www.diverseeducators.co.uk/our-dei-glossary/

Director Characteristics, Gender Balance and Insolvency Risk: An Empirical Study (Wilson, N. & Ali, A., 2009) - https://www.researchgate.net/publication/228299596_Director_Characteristics_Gender_Balance_and_Insolvency_Risk_An_Empirical_Study

Diversify: An award-winning guide to why inclusion is better for everyone (June Sarpong, 2019) - https://amzn.to/4614aNZ

Diversity wins, (McKinsey, 2019) - https://www.mckinsey.com/featured-insights/diversity-and-inclusion/diversity-wins-how-inclusion-matters

Diversity, Equity and Inclusion for Dummies (Dr. Shirley Davis, 2022) - https://amzn.to/3ZsweHq

Firms with more women in the c-suite are more profitable (Nolan & Moran, 2016) - https://hbr.org/2016/02/study-firms-with-more-women-in-the-c-suite-are-more-profitable

Gender diversity within R&D teams: Its impact on radicalness of innovation, (Cristina Díaz-García, Angela González-Moreno & Francisco Jose Sáez-Martínez, 2013) - https://www.researchgate.net/publication/274777911_Gender_diversity_within_RD_teams_Its_impact_on_radicalness_of_innovation

Groupthink: Definition, Signs, Examples and How to Avoid It - verywellmind.com - https://www.verywellmind.com/what-is-groupthink-2795213

How Groupthink Can Cost Your Business - Entrepreneur Magazine - https://www.entrepreneur.com/leadership/how-group think-can-cost-your-business-and-3-corporate/311864

Inclusive Leadership: The Definitive Guide to Developing and Executing an Impactful Diversity and Inclusion Strategy - (Charlotte Sweeny and Fleur Bothwick) - https://amzn.to/46ijcOU

Intellectual Humility (Shane Snow) - https://shanesnow.com/deci sion-making-skills

Mindset: Changing The Way You think To Fulfil Your Potential (Carol Dweck, 2017) - https://amzn.to/47fa6TV

Psychology Today - Why Diverse Teams Outperform Homogeneous Teams - https://www.psychologytoday.com/us/blog/your-brain-work/202106/why-diverse-teams-outperform-homoge neous-teams

Social Support and the Perception of Geographical (Slant Schall et al, 2008) - https://www.researchgate.net/publication/222394512_Social_Support_and_the_Perception_of_Geographi cal_Slant

The Fearless Organization: Creating Psychological Safety in the Workplace for Learning, Innovation, and Growth (Amy Edmondson, 2018) - https://amzn.to/3FpH08i

The Key to Inclusion: A Practical Guide to Diversity, Equity and Belonging for You, Your Team and Your Organization (Edited by Stephen Frost, 2022) - https://amzn.to/48S8XTE

The Most Admired Companies are More Global Than Ever - Fortune Magazine - https://fortune.com/2015/02/19/wmac-glob alization2-0/

The Role of Gender in Team Collaboration and Performance (Bear & Woolley, 2011) - https://www.researchgate.net/publication/ 228196582_The_Role_of_Gender_in_Team_Collabora tion_and_Performance

The Secret Resume Podcast - The Secret Resume | a podcast by Melody Moore, Liberare Consulting (podbean.com)

The Too-Much-Talent Effect: Team Interdependence Determines When More Talent Is Too Much Versus Not Enough (Swaab et al, 2014) - https://www.researchgate.net/publication/ 261713192_The_Too-Much-Talent_Effect_Team_Interdepen dence_Determines_When_More_Talent_Is_Too_Much_Ver sus_Not_Enough_Draft_Version

Toward gender parity: Women on boards initiative research report (Bourne et al, 2016) - https://www.publications.qld.gov.au/ dataset/60f7ba5f-f718-45bd-981e-2e045dd43991/resource/ 88548033-c10a-44ab-b3a2-ec5ecea48212/download/toward-gender-parity-women-boards-research-report-full.pdf

Training Magazine Research: Work Team Training And Perfor-mance Gaps - https://trainingmag.com/work-team-training-and-performance-gaps/

PART ONE

THE INCLUSIVE TEAM™ MODEL

"Great things in business are never done by one person; they're done by a team of people."

— STEVE JOBS

CHAPTER 1

TRUST

"Great teams consist of individuals who have learned to trust each other. Over time, they have discovered each other's strengths and weaknesses, enabling them to play as a coordinated whole."

— *AMY EDMONSON*

WHY IS TRUST IMPORTANT?

From an organisational perspective, the benefits of trusting and being trusted are clear. Research by Paul J Zak found that employees in high-trust organisations are more productive, collaborate better, have more energy, are happier with their lives, suffer less chronic stress, and stay with their employers longer than those with low-trust employers. *Training* magazine research found survey respondents identified trust in other team members as the number one factor in determining the amount of effort the respondents put into a team.

Trust is essential if team members are to cooperate and collaborate towards team goals. Researchers Adebayo Agbejule and colleagues suggest that it leads to increased creativity and team learning. They also talk about the difference between vertical trust (trust between the team and the team leader) and horizontal trust (the trust between team members) which is a useful way of thinking about it, as high performing teams need both.

We explored in the introduction that humans are born vulnerable. We rely on others to take care of us and ensure our survival. We are biologically programmed to be part of a pack or a tribe, and we need to be able to trust the members of our tribe to protect us and put the needs of the tribe above their individual desires.

However, whilst we are naturally inclined to trust each other, we don't always do so and there will be varying degrees of trust between team members.

We are more likely to trust people who are similar to us in some way, and who are members of our own social group. This is often known as the in-group/out-group phenomenon or similarity bias. The effect is so strong that even if we are randomly assigned to a small group, it is enough to create a sense of in-group and change our behaviour towards the out-group.

We tend to treat members of our in-group better – we are more empathetic and judge them less harshly. This a potential problem in a diverse team, where we are more likely to trust and engage with the team members who are more like us. This could result in exclusion of some team members and a sense of in-group/out-group within the team.

Fortunately, the sense of in/out-group is relatively fluid, and by creating a sense of in-group throughout the team we can start to build trust even among very different team members. You can learn more about this in the Team Identity section of the Alignment chapter.

PSYCHOLOGICAL SAFETY AND TRUST

Psychological safety is defined by Dr Amy Edmondson, who researched and popularised this term, as 'a belief that one will not be punished or humiliated for speaking up with ideas, questions, concerns or mistakes, and that the team is safe for interpersonal risk-taking'. She found that psychological safety predicts both group learning and performance: teams that feel safe learn and perform better.

It intuitively makes sense. Team and individual growth require us to stretch ourselves and leave our comfort zones. If we feel that we are in an unsafe environment where we will be punished or ridiculed for trying something new or for failing, then we are more likely to not bother trying. If we feel safe and know that our efforts will be met with support and encouragement, we are more likely to try something new or things we perceive as risky. The behaviours included in The Inclusive Team™ model are designed to create a feeling of psychological safety in the team.

NEUROSCIENCE OF TRUST

Neuroscientists have been studying what happens in the brain when we trust or don't trust people.

They found that higher levels of oxytocin are related to a reduction in the fear of trusting a stranger, a reduction in social anxiety and an increased motivation to cooperate with and help each other.

If we are under too much stress or feel threatened in some way, oxytocin tends to be inhibited, which means we tend to trust less and find it more difficult to interact and collaborate with others effectively.

Conversely, levels of oxytocin are increased through means such as recognising high performance, setting challenging but achievable goals, developing people (see Growth chapter for more on these), empowering individuals (see below) and building relationships (see Respect chapter). The higher levels of oxytocin created more trust in teams.

The Inclusive Team™ model places a strong focus on building an environment where people feel positive, valued and safe. This increases people's oxytocin levels and thus levels of both horizontal and vertical trust in the team.

TRUST CLUSTER

There are two sub-clusters in the Trust Cluster, the first of which is Empowerment – are all team members empowered to do their job and do they trust each other? The second sub-cluster is Conflict – are team members comfortable sharing their views, asking 'stupid' questions and dealing with healthy conflict?

SUB-CLUSTER: EMPOWERMENT

This sub-cluster has three key elements: equal opportunities, streamlined processes and trust between team members.

Equal Opportunities

This means that the leader delegates important tasks across the team and doesn't have favourites who tend to get all the exciting opportunities. All team members, therefore, have significant responsibilities.

What we tend to see is that team leaders have 'go-to people' or favourites (I like to call them 'point people') who they trust to get things done. They allocate more of the high risk, exciting work (or stretch assignments) to those team members. These team members build their skills by being stretched, and often increase their visibility in the organisation. It becomes a positive reinforcing loop or upwards spiral.

The problem is that the team leader tends to trust people similar to them – they are in the team leader's in-group. People who are less similar to the team leader tend not to be given the stretch assignments, don't get the opportunity to prove themselves, and therefore are not considered for future stretch assignments. It is a downward spiral or negative reinforcing loop.

I'm sure we have all seen this happen in a highly visible way: a leader 'adopts' a younger member of the team who becomes their protegee; they are taken to important meetings, introduced to senior people and involved in important and interesting work. Often this person is a 'mini-me' of the leader: they look like them, they act like them, and they thrive because of the opportunities they are given. At the same time, other, equally competent colleagues feel left out, frustrated and like they will never catch a break.

However, many other less visible or extreme examples exist in every team. We are all guilty of trusting and relying on certain team members more than others, or hesitating to take a risk on people we don't know so well.

The converse to this is also true: under-represented team members tend to volunteer for and be asked to take on many of the 'low value' team tasks. You know the type of things – arranging a conference, serving on a committee, taking notes in a meeting. I call them 'office housekeeping', and it is one of my pet peeves that the events to celebrate certain DEI dates (e.g., International Women's Day, Black History Month) are often organised by the very people they are supposed to be celebrating. It feels like having to organise your own birthday party.

It's not that these tasks don't add value. They often contribute to the smooth running of the organisation or the creation of a particular culture, but they are not the kind of thing people get recognised or promoted for. A 2018 HBR article (see references) looked at this from the perspective of gender, and it chimes with my own experience. For example, when I recently worked with a group of Employee Resource Group (ERG) heads, I noticed that around ninety percent of them were women.

In an inclusive high performing team, responsibilities and stretch assignments will be more widely spread among team members, giving a broader range of people the opportunity to develop and prove themselves and to take on their fair share of the office housekeeping.

Streamlined Processes

The second element of empowerment is the need for team members to be trusted to get on with their work without the constraints of unnecessary bureaucracy or checking for approval. Some organisations and sectors may be more bureaucratic than others (hello, UK public sector!) but it is important to minimise this as much as possible within a team to give individuals the freedom to take calculated risks and make decisions without constantly having to seek approval from someone more senior.

I have seen great examples of high and low levels of trust in this area. The first was when I worked for a Canadian ski company in Whistler in the late 1990s. Having come from working for the UK National Health Service, which was intensely bureaucratic, I was really impressed with the ski company's approach to customer service and in particular dealing with customer complaints. Customer facing staff were empowered both to be themselves (Juggling bottles in the bar? Go for it. Singing a song whilst shovelling snow? Sure, why not.) and to deal with customer complaints on the spot. This meant they could give out free drinks to compensate for mistakes or give a cookie to a child because they were crying. Obviously, there were guidelines and limits, but basically, they were trusted not to game the system, and were enabled to rapidly and instantly deal with a problem before it became a big issue. Customers were kept happy, and management time wasn't wasted dealing with simple to fix problems because they were dealt with at source and didn't tend to get escalated.

At the other end of the scale was a large sales team I worked with that had to have every deal (no matter how large or small) signed off by their manager's boss – let's call him Jim. This lack of trust led to a chronically over-worked Jim, frustrated salespeople, delays in sales and irritated customers. When a new leader replaced Jim, she couldn't believe what she was seeing, and instantly created a more streamlined system where only the larger deals required her sign off. This led to a significantly less frustrated team, a quicker sales process and increased business because the salespeople had more time to focus on their customers rather than getting bogged down in lengthy sign off processes. There is an exercise at the end of this chapter that will help your team identify and remove processes and bureaucracy that get in the way of them performing at their best.

Trust Between Team Members

We have a tendency to more readily trust people who are like us, but an inclusive high performing team will have high degrees of trust between all the team members, regardless of whether they are alike or not.

This is known as horizonal trust. It means that we believe people do what they say they are doing and that they are capable, reliable and responsible. This enables us to focus on what we need to do without having to worry about whether other important aspects of the team's work are being completed.

This is particularly important when there are interdependencies: if we are reliant on one part of the team to do their work before we can do ours, and we trust them to do it, this reduces anxiety and frees up our mental capacity to focus and innovate in our own areas.

SUB-CLUSTER: CONFLICT

The second sub-cluster of Trust is the presence of healthy conflict. When I first read Patrick Lencioni's *The Five Dysfunctions of a Team* about twenty years ago, the key thing that stood out for me was the benefit of conflict in a team. I was already working as a consultant, and had some experience of delivering team building workshops, which tended to focus on getting to know each other's personality preferences and work style as a way of building relationships and improving team performance. I am also someone who tends to avoid conflict, so I found the idea that it could have a positive impact on team performance both challenging and fascinating.

I learnt from Lencioni that focusing too much on harmony or agreement is actually unhelpful to a team as people then tend to not share their ideas if they are different from those of other members of the team. Whilst this may feel more comfortable and allow the team atmosphere to remain collegiate, it means that the team will not air potentially helpful ideas or different perspectives.

This may result in poor decisions and is one of the main causes of groupthink (see Introduction for more on this).

If one of the aims of a team is to benefit from the collective intelligence, it is important that *all* views are heard and considered. This is particularly important with diverse teams, where the benefits of diversity of experience and thought will be missed if everyone does not feel able to share their perspectives. A high performing inclusive team needs to encourage the sharing of ideas and build their comfort with conflict – they need to become comfortable with being uncomfortable!

The Conflict sub-cluster has two main elements: firstly, the encouragement of people to speak up and the expectation that they will; secondly, it being ok to not know the answer.

Speaking Up

This is the *encouragement* of team members to speak up and share their ideas and perspectives, particularly if they are different from those of other members of the team. This is not just the team leader's task, but one shared by all team members. It is important that others are encouraged to share, and also that team members listen to one another. There needs to be an understanding that conflict may occur, and that it shouldn't be avoided or difficult discussions closed down.

A study by Anita Woolley and colleagues found that teams in which people speak in roughly equal amounts far outperform those in which one or two people dominate the conversation.

However, it is also important to acknowledge that not everybody enjoys speaking up in a team meeting. For instance, some people may lack confidence speaking in groups or they may suffer from impostor syndrome. Some people who are neurodivergent or have a preference for Introversion may also not find it easy to speak up in a group situation.

You should be striving to create a psychologically safe team environment where even people who find it difficult are able to contribute in group settings. At the same time, you can ensure that people who find it more challenging also have other ways of contributing to team discussions and decisions. For instance, individuals might brainstorm onto post-its (sticky notes), which are then put on the wall and clustered. You might speak to people before a meeting and ask for their thoughts. You might specifically invite them by name to share their perspective. The solutions will be unique to the individuals and the team and should be explored with those concerned.

I see this as both parties adapting and collaborating to find a way that works well both for the individuals and the team. The exercise you will find in the Respect chapter that focuses on developing the Diversity sub-cluster is helpful in surfacing these types of challenges and solutions.

Closely linked to the encouragement of people to speak up is the *expectation* that team members will speak up – an understanding that being part of the team means you contribute, even if it's not your area of expertise. I remember coaching a member of a senior leadership team and had a great deal of expertise in his subject matter. He tended to stay silent when the team discussed anything he didn't think was part of his remit, even when he had a point of view.

He was surprised to discover in his 360 feedback that his peers were asking for him to speak up more: they really respected him and his way of looking at the world, and wanted his perspective, even when on matters outside his area of expertise. This information and a conversation about what being an enterprise leader really meant led to a mindset shift and complete transformation of how he behaved in the leadership team meetings. A change in self-image from functional leader (responsible for his own area) to enterprise leader (responsible for the whole organisation) gave him permission to behave in a different way which had a positive impact on him and the team.

It's Ok to not Know

The second element of the Conflict sub-cluster is that it needs to be ok to not know – to not be the expert on everything and to share a perspective even if it is not fully formed. Team members must feel able to share half formed ideas, ask 'stupid' questions or acknowledge that they don't understand something. Believing we don't have to know everything, and it is ok to let other people know that is an aspect of growth mindset and intellectual humility. (See the Adaptability chapter for more on intellectual humility and the Growth chapter for more on growth mindset.)

I have done a lot of work with the UK Civil Service, and my experience is that they have a culture in which it is hard to admit when they don't know something. As an example, I was doing a piece of evaluation research and my client suggested that we didn't ask too many questions of the key stakeholders so that it wouldn't look like we didn't know what we were doing.

As an outsider to the organisation, I didn't share her fear of being seen as incompetent for asking a lot of questions. My approach had been to ask as many questions as possible, because that way we could collect a wide range of perspectives to help us identify clear recommendations. I was looking for data; she was trying to maintain her reputation.

If team members feel a strong pressure to always behave as though they know the answer, to only put forward fully formed ideas and not ask questions to find out more information, the team's ability to collaborate and innovate will be seriously impacted.

In inclusive high performing teams, there are no stupid questions; team members can be vulnerable and admit there are gaps in their knowledge because they don't fear that their competence will be judged. This reduces the probability that decisions will be made on half-truths and assumptions. It increases the team's ability to innovate and build on each other's ideas.

Everyday Actions to Build Trust in Your Team – for Team Members

- Think about who your 'point people' are in the team. Who do you choose to spend time with/seek the advice of/trust/choose to work with? How different from or similar to you are they? Could you expand that group of 'point people'?
- Monitor how much you speak up in group situations. Are you holding back? Can you speak up more, even if you find it difficult?
- Pay attention to how much others speak in group situations. Do some people dominate the conversation? Can you ask the quieter members for their perspective and ensure they get recognised for their contribution?
- What is your conflict style? How might you adjust your style to encourage healthy conflict in the team?
- Encourage risk taking in the team. Know your own risk profile, and if you have a low tolerance for risk, make sure you don't habitually block innovations.
- Keep to your word. Build trust by being reliable and doing what you say you will.

- Ask 'stupid' questions. Don't be afraid to admit that you don't know or understand something – you may find that you are not the only one. And your 'stupid' question may expose something that hasn't been thought of or an assumption that has been made.
- Spend time getting to know and building trusted relationships with your colleagues.
- Make sure you take on your fair share of 'office housekeeping'.

Everyday Actions to Build Trust in Your Team – for Team Leaders

- Think about who your 'point people' are. Do you seek the perspective of delegating/providing opportunities across the team or only to some? Can you expand your pool of 'point people'?
- Make sure 'office housekeeping' is shared equally across the team.
- Keep to your word. Don't commit to things you are not sure you can deliver.
- Look out for people who abuse your trust or the trust of other team members. Hold those people to account.
- Take time to understand your personal strengths and development areas regarding trust. How comfortable are you with trusting people? Could you trust more?
- Delegate authority and decision making to your team. Don't make them constantly seek your approval or sign off.
- Review the processes and structures in your team. Are they helping or hindering? What can you do to reduce the

bureaucracy or poor behaviours that get in the way of the team performing at their best?

- Take time to reflect on your own appetite for risk. Are you overly cautious? Do you make it ok for the team to take calculated risks? Make sure you are not having a negative impact on the team.

- Pay attention to vertical trust *and* horizontal trust. That is, do the team trust *you*, and is there trust between the team members? What can you do to help develop it?

- Monitor who speaks the most and least in meetings. Invite people to speak and stop the most vocal members dominating the conversation.

- Take time to understand your personal strengths and development areas regarding conflict. How comfortable are you with conflict? Do you tend to shut down conflict? You may find it helpful to take a survey like the Thomas-Kilmann Conflict Mode Instrument (TKI) to understand your conflict style (see references).

- Clarify your expectations about contributions to the team. Make it clear that you expect them to contribute ideas and share their perspectives.

- Get to know your team. Why don't the quieter members speak up? What can you do to help them speak up in group situations? In what ways can they contribute their views outside of group meetings?

- Openly encourage a 'there are no stupid questions' mindset. State that it is important. Role model by asking the stupid questions yourself.

- Keep track of commitments and hold people to account. Build trust by ensuring people keep to their word.

- Focus on creating a team climate where people don't feel constantly under threat, and where oxytocin (the feel-good hormone) is produced. This will help create a climate of trust – see 'The Neuroscience of Trust' article in the references for more on this.

Two Questions to Measure Trust in Your Team

You can ask your team members to score the team using two questions. Ask them to give scores from one (Never) to five (Always).

1. Do the team trust each other and feel empowered to do their work without too much unnecessary bureaucracy?
2. Do the team feel encouraged to speak up and that differences of opinion are welcome?

Team Development Exercises to Develop Trust in Your Team

Here are two exercises you can use with your team to develop the Trust cluster. The first is for Empowerment and the second is for Conflict. You can facilitate them yourself or ask a member of the team to do it. See Chapter Six for further information about facilitating team exercises.

Trust Cluster: Empowerment Exercise

'Room 101' Activity

High performing inclusive teams are not just engaged, they are enabled and empowered to perform. The purpose of this activity is to explore and plan to eliminate the things that get in the way of the team doing their best work.

This exercise is not designed to become a moaning session: the team must identify blockers and come up with ways to do something about them. Strong facilitation may be required to help the team focus on suggesting changes and improvement and stop them getting caught up in criticism.

The exercise also develops behaviours from other clusters such as Alignment (helping the team feel accountable for the team performance; involving them in the development of plans), Growth (focus on continuous improvement; paying attention to the way the team works together), and Adaptability (bringing new ideas to the group).

You can download this exercise and the team member handout via the Liberare Consulting website – a link can be found at the back of the book.

Team Pre-work – estimated time 20-30 minutes:

1. Share the 'Room 101' handout with the team and ask them to complete it in advance of the session.
2. Ensure the team know they will be discussing the pre-work in the team session, so it is important they complete it beforehand and bring it to the session with them.

Facilitator Pre-work – estimated time 60 minutes:

1. Complete the handout yourself so you can share your thoughts in the workshop, but also so you can answer the team's questions when they are filling it out.
2. Re-read the chapter on Trust to remind yourself why you are doing this exercise, and to identify the key messages you want to share with the team.

At the Team Session – 5 minutes intro, 25 minutes activity, 15 minutes debrief

Introduce the reason for the activity (5 minutes)

The purpose of the session is to identify behaviours or processes that the team feel get in the way of them doing the best job they can: what they would like to put into Room 101. Room 101 comes from the book *1984* by George Orwell, which you can explain if people haven't heard of it. It is where we would put away our pet peeves and all the things that really irritate us. When things go into Room 101, they can never come out.

For example, people might feel that they constantly have to seek approval or deal with unnecessary bureaucracy. One of the important elements of being a high performing and inclusive team is that the team members feel trusted and empowered to carry out their work without this.

The twist is that if they are going to remove something they must come up with a better idea: they have to replace it with something.

Remind them about and get agreement to confidentiality. What is discussed in the room stays in the room. They can share their personal story and experience outside the room, but they should not share anything that anyone else has said or done.

Start the activity (25 minutes)

Split the team into groups of around four.

Ask them to go round the group and each share the top two things they believe should go into Room 101. Ask them to describe not only the thing that annoys them, but the impact it has and the solution they propose. Remind them it is not an opportunity to moan, but to come up with ideas and solutions to help the team work more effectively.

When everyone has shared, they should discuss the suggestions and agree on two things to share with the main group. Ask them to nominate a spokesperson to say what they want to go into Room 101 and what should replace it.

As the facilitator you do not join a group. You can check they understand the instructions, but do not get drawn into the discussion. This is particularly important if you are also the team leader, as it would be very easy for you to become the focus of the conversation, rather than the ideas and perspectives of the group.

Debrief as a group (15 minutes)

Get each group to share the top two things they believe should go into Room 101. If they focus too much on how frustrating the thing is, prompt them to answer the three other questions in the worksheet:

- What impact does it have on their work?
- How could it be improved?
- How will that make things better?

Facilitate a discussion about which ones are the key priorities for the whole group. Get the group to vote on the top two that will have the most impact and that you (collectively) think you have an influence on. Get them to think about the circles of concern, influence and control (see picture below – you could draw it up for them on a flipchart).

Concern

Influence

Control

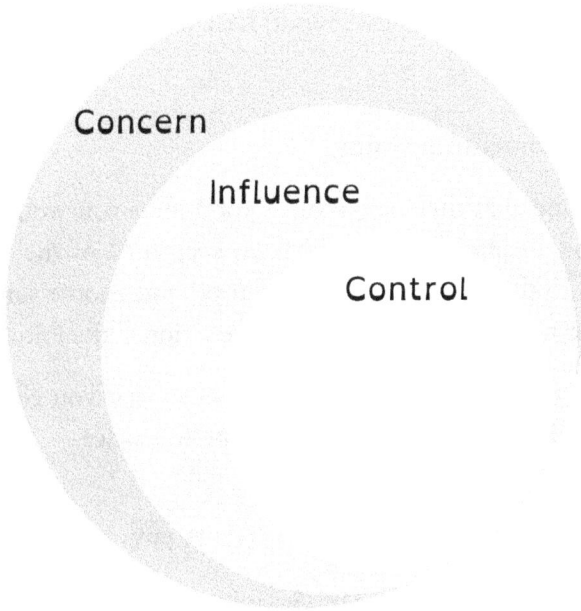

You can control some things, and you can influence some things, but some things you can neither control nor influence. They are in your circle of concern. Try to focus on things you can either directly control or are confident you have influence over.

Once you have chosen your top two, create a quick high level action plan and implementation team for each one. The aim is not to get into the detail, but to create a mini project team who take ownership of the activity. Use the GARU model to help you plan:

- Goal – what have you decided needs to be done? What is your goal?
- Action – what action(s) need to take place in order to achieve this?
- Responsibility – who is going to take responsibility for making it happen? Who else will be involved?

- Update – when will they report back on their progress to the wider team?

Keep the Momentum Going

You may find that there are a lot of good ideas you would like to implement. Ensure that you/the team keep hold of the materials generated so that you can re-visit the topic and choose some more blockers to take action on once you have actioned the initial ones.

Carry out this exercise on a regular basis so that you continually identify and eliminate blockers to team performance.

Trust Cluster: Conflict Activity

'What Conflict Means to Me' Activity

The purpose of this activity is to explore what conflict means to individuals in the team and to help the team understand that healthy conflict is to be expected and welcomed in a diverse and inclusive high performing team.

The exercise also develops behaviours found in other clusters such as Alignment (helping the team feel accountable for the team performance; involving them in the development of plans), and Growth (focus on continuous improvement; paying attention to the way the team works together).

You can download this exercise and the team member handout via the Liberare Consulting website – a link can be found at the back of the book.

Team Member Pre-work – estimated time 30 minutes:

1. Share the 'What Conflict Means to Me' handout with the team and ask them to complete it in advance of the session.
2. Ensure the team know they will be discussing the pre-work in the team session, so it is important they complete it beforehand and bring it to the session with them.

Facilitator Pre-work – estimated time 60 minutes:

1. Make sure you complete the handout yourself so you can share your thoughts in the workshop, but also so you can answer the team's questions when they are filling it out.
2. Re-read the chapter on Trust to remind yourself why you are doing this exercise, and to identify the key messages you want to share with the team.

At the team session – 5 minutes intro, 20 minutes activity, 20 minutes debrief

Introduce the reason for the activity (5 minutes)

The purpose of the session is to explore the role of conflict in team performance. It is possible that the more diverse a team is, the more likely conflict is to occur.

It is helpful if every individual understands how they feel about conflict and works out ways to ensure they can disagree with each other in a way that helps them perform better as a team.

Remind them about and get agreement to confidentiality. What is discussed in the room stays in the room. They can share their personal story and experience outside the room, but they should not share anything that anyone else has said or done.

Start the activity (20 minutes)

Split the teams into small groups. This discussion can be quite challenging so smaller groups of around three are best.

Explain that they have two tasks in their small groups:

1. Share their responses to the pre-work questions including which conflict styles they thought were their defaults.
2. Discuss how they feel conflict is handled in the team. How can things be improved to ensure different voices are heard? How do you ensure healthy conflict?
3. Ask them to nominate a spokesperson to share back key themes.

As the facilitator, you do not go into any of the small groups. You can wander around and check in to see if they have any questions, but do not get drawn into a long conversation with any group.

Debrief as a group (20 minutes)

Write 'Conflict Styles' at the top of a flip chart and the names of the conflict styles down the left-hand side. As they return to the main group, ask the team members to put a tick (check mark) next to their top two default styles. They don't need to put their names – you just want to see if there are patterns in the group.

Go round the small groups and ask for the key themes from their discussions.

Encourage them to understand that conflict is not simply 'bad'. If done in the right way it is just a result of diverse perspectives being shared.

As a group, look at the team's default styles on the flipchart. What does it tell you about the team? Are any of the styles over- or under-represented? What does that mean for you as a team?

Ask the group what they think the difference is between healthy and unhealthy conflict.

Write 'Rules for Healthy Conflict' on the flip chart and get the group to brainstorm the behaviours they believe are essential for healthy conflict in the team. Remember, there are no right or wrong answers – it is about deciding what is right for your team. Confirm with the group that they agree these are the rules they will sign up to.

Decide how you are going to use the rules and what you are going to do with them. For instance, you may have them up on the wall in your office or bring them to team meetings. I have even seen some teams do creative things like getting them printed on mugs.

At the end of the session, ask each team member to reflect and write down how they personally are going to behave differently as a result of the conversations they have had.

Keep the Momentum Going

Ensure the rules are kept where you can see them. If you are a virtual team you may need to be more creative.

You can use the rules as a reminder at the start of a meeting or at a time you think the team are being too agreeable and not speaking their minds.

Review the rules with the team occasionally to evaluate the team behaviours against the rules, to decide if they are still relevant or need updating.

REFERENCES

Evidence for a Collective Intelligence Factor in the Performance of Human Groups (Woolley et al, 2010) - https://www.researchgate.net/publication/47369848_Evidence_of_a_Collective_Intelligence_Factor_in_the_Performance_of_Human_Groups

The Five Dysfunctions of a Team (Patrick Lencioni, 2002) - https://amzn.to/46OfIUY

The Neuroscience of Trust (Paul J Zak, 2017) - https://hbr.org/2017/01/the-neuroscience-of-trust

The Thomas-Kilmann Conflict Inventory - https://eu.themyersbriggs.com/en/tools/TKI

Why Women Volunteer for Tasks That Don't Lead to Promotions (Linda Babcock, Maria P. Recalde, and Lise Vesterlund, 2018) - https://hbr.org/2018/07/why-women-volunteer-for-tasks-that-dont-lead-to-promotions

CHAPTER 2

ALIGNMENT

"The way the team plays as a whole determines its success. You may have the greatest bunch of individual stars in the world, but if they don't play together, the club won't be worth a dime."

— *BABE RUTH*

WHY IS ALIGNMENT IMPORTANT?

Alignment is an absolutely fundamental concept for organisations. In its simplest terms it means that the vision and strategy are clear, and that people are pulling in the same direction, rather than following their own path. A useful analogy is of people in a rowing boat: if they all pull together at the same time, in the same direction, the boat will move smoothly. If, however, one or more of them does not pull so hard, or their timing is different from everyone else's, or they don't agree on their direction, the boat will slow down, may go round in circles or may fail to reach its destination.

In The Inclusive Team™ model there are two sub-clusters to Alignment: first is the Direction the team is going in – does the team share a sense of direction, purpose and vision and do they know who is responsible for specific goals? The second is Account-ability – does the team feel a sense of shared responsibility for the development and achievement of team goals? Do they believe in the power of the team and collaborate effectively?

SUB-CLUSTER: DIRECTION

A number of factors make up our Direction sub-cluster. Does the team have clarity of vision, mission and purpose? Is there a shared team identity? And is there a clear structure and lines of respon-sibility?

A quick Google search will show you that the terms *vision, mission, purpose* and *strategy* are defined in different ways yet are often used interchangeably and sometimes combined. For clarity, I define the terms in the following way:

Vision – Where is the team going? What is the direction of travel and what does the future look like? This tends to be written in a future focused way.

Mission – What you are trying to achieve and for whom. This tends to be more action focused.

Purpose – Why your team exists. What meaningful impact are you trying to have? I find that the purpose typically represents the shared values of the team.

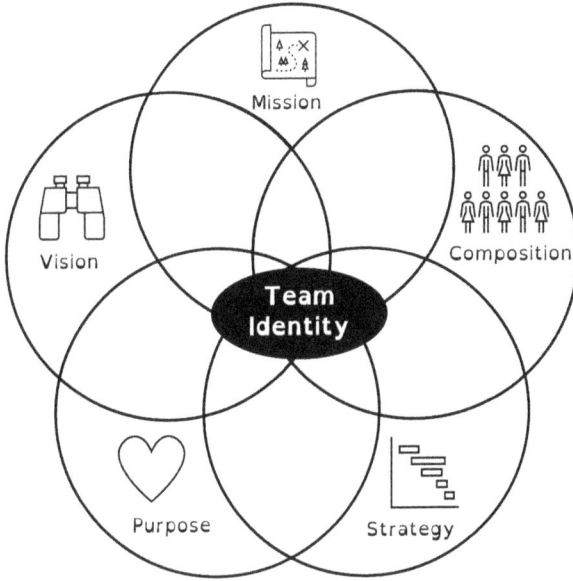

Strategy – This captures the goals and high level plans that will allow you to achieve your vision, mission and purpose.

When we add in *team composition* (who is in the team) these five elements create the team identity.

Clarity of Direction

My experience is that team members often *think* they are aligned on the team purpose, vision, etc., but in reality, they all have slightly different (and sometimes radically diverse) views. A McKinsey article gives an example of an energy company where five top team executives were asked to list the company's ten highest priorities. They listed twenty-three in total – with only two appearing on every executive's list. I smiled when I read it, because it chimed with my experience with teams.

Clarity of direction is one of the most important elements of team performance. If the team members don't understand why the team exists – where they are going and how they support the organisation's aims – they are likely to be pulling in different directions. This is particularly important in the VUCA post-Covid world. The context in which the team works changes regularly and quickly, and high levels of ambiguity increase the probability that people will interpret things in different ways and have a range of opinions about the desired direction for the team.

In addition, teams often operate in a virtual or hybrid way. The reduction in the time the team spends together can increase the opportunity for miscommunication and lack of clarity. The *Training* magazine research I mentioned in the introduction identified a lack of clarity among team members as the number one obstacle to team performance.

The assumption of alignment means that teams rarely question or discuss the vision, and they often act individually and make decisions based on their different interpretations. A high performing team will ensure that clarity of direction is established and consistently referred to, firstly to ensure that the direction is still the right one and secondly to ensure that everyone is still clear and aligned to the direction.

There is an interesting explanation from the neuroscience world as to why each team member has their own perspective on the team's direction, which is that the human brain craves clarity and certainty. Uncertainty lights up the areas of the brain in a way similar to actual physical pain. When we encounter ambiguity or confusion, we tend to try to create our own clarity in order to avoid the pain of uncertainty. In the absence of clarity around goals and vision in the team, individuals make up their own version in order to reduce their feelings of discomfort. They then act in accordance with their own version.

To compound matters, once people have created clarity for themselves, it can be difficult to change perspective when confronted with contradictory information. They experience cognitive dissonance and will perform complex mental gymnastics to ensure their world view is not threatened. (See Adaptability chapter for more on this.)

Mission and Purpose

A great direction that team members can coalesce around will not just state 'what' the team are trying to do, but also 'why' they are doing it: what impact is the team trying to have?

The team members need to understand why the team exists in the first place. What can they collectively uniquely achieve that each of them operating individually cannot achieve? The introduction outlined the difference between a team and a work group – a group only really becomes a team if it has a unique purpose. If the team don't understand and align to this purpose, they are likely to prioritise achieving their own individual goals above those of the team.

There has been a recent increase in interest in the understanding of the importance of purpose and how it motivates and engages employees to help achieve the organisation's aims. This is about establishing not just what the organisation wants to achieve (goals and targets), but *why* you want to do it – what impact do you aim to have? Purpose typically extends beyond financial goals and metrics and is more aligned to values. I think of goals and targets as the 'head' and purpose as the 'heart'.

The clothing brand Patagonia is a good example of a purpose driven businesses. They state that, 'Patagonia is in business to save our home planet.' Since 1985 they have pledged one percent of total sales to the 'preservation and restoration of the natural environment'.

Research suggests this is good for business. Deloitte says that purpose driven companies report forty percent higher levels of workforce retention, and recent McKinsey research found that seventy percent of employees said their sense of purpose is defined by their work. Accenture suggest that 62 percent of consumers want companies to stand up for the issues they are passionate about, and 66 percent think transparency is one of a brand's most attractive qualities.

From the perspective of the individual, a study in the journal *Psychosomatic Medicine* found that when people have a greater sense of purpose, they have lower mortality and a reduced incidence of cardiovascular disease. The Rush Memory and Aging Project found that patients who have a sense of purpose are 2.5 times more likely to be free of dementia and 22 percent less likely to exhibit risk factors for stroke.

You may also have come across the concept of the 'Blue Zones' which Dan Buettner wrote about in his book of the same name (you'll find a link to his TED talk in the references). There are five blue zones in the world: geographic areas with lower rates of chronic disease and a longer life expectancy. One of the nine factors the researchers found in common between people in the different zones was *purpose* – a reason to get out of bed in the morning... or Ikigai as the Japanese residents of Okinawa call it.

A team purpose doesn't have to be as far-reaching as the Patagonia statement, but it does need to be clear, inspiring and give the team something to align with. The real magic comes when the team purpose aligns strongly with the purpose felt by the individual team members – not only do they have clarity of direction, but a strong emotional connection to the team's work.

The exercise at the end of this chapter will help you and your team identify and articulate your team purpose.

Team Composition

The team composition may seem simple. It is who the team members are, and why they are in the team.

However, surprisingly often I have worked with teams that seem to have permeable boundaries – different people turn up to team meetings, and nobody knows who is officially in the team and who is not. This is often the case when a team is made up of the direct reports of an individual, particularly when the team leader oversees a number of different, sometimes unrelated, areas. They don't actually have a shared goal, and because of this I would say they are a work group not a team.

I once ran a team away day for a CEO who had an enormous top team of people who were her direct reports and some of *their* direct reports. The away day helped her realise they weren't really a team, and immediately after the workshop she rationalised the size of the team to a more manageable number of people who could more easily work together towards a shared goal.

It can be a difficult conversation for a team leader to have, but just because someone is your direct report doesn't mean they should be part of your team. If your mission, vision, direction, strategy and purpose are clear, the team should be composed of the people who need to work together to achieve that goal. I frequently see teams in which the majority of the team have an impact on the goal, but one or two team members have a role that is not related and do not really add value as a team member.

Sometimes team leaders will have two teams: a smaller, real team that collaborate to achieve shared goals, and a larger one (in reality a work group) that get together to communicate and coordinate. (See the Accountability sub-cluster later in this chapter for more on the differences between collaboration, coordination and communication.)

Team Identity

The team identity is a combination of the vision, mission, purpose, strategy and composition. It answers the questions of *who is this team?* and *why do they exist?*

As stated in previous chapters, we are social, tribal creatures with a strong need to belong which is beneficial to our survival. Interestingly, another of the nine longevity factors that the blue zones research found was 'the right tribe'. Strong social networks also play a role in keeping us alive for longer. The team identity lets us know we are in a team and why that team exists.

This can be particularly important for diverse teams because we all have a sense of in-groups and out-groups, which are typically based on people who are like us. We are more likely to consider people who look, sound and behave like us as our in-group and people who are different as the out-group. As we explored in the Trust chapter, we tend to trust and favour members of our in-group, and our brains are less likely to be in a defensive state. We are more likely to listen to them, pay attention to them, and support their ideas.

Additionally, if we don't feel like we belong (when we are placed in the out-group by others) our brains will be in a cautious threat state. As we discussed in the introduction, the more threat our brains perceive, the less access we have to positive resources such as focus, resilience, collaboration, and creativity. Therefore, if you have a diverse team who don't look, sound or behave like one another, the team may not feel safe or trust each other easily and may be in a constant physiological state of threat. This is inevitably going to have a negative effect on team performance.

The good news is that the category of in-group and out-group is surprisingly fluid. We can create the sense of in-group by creating a shared purpose or group identity and helping team members focus on what they have in common. Research suggests that even highly selfish people can become more cooperative if they identify with the in-group, and that creating a sense of in-group can help overcome some of the biases and challenges that normally occur when working with diverse team members.

The creation of a strong team identity allows the perception of threat to reduce, giving team members access to more positive mental states (empathy, resilience, collaboration, innovation, etc.), meaning that diverse teams can profit from the unique contributions of the team members. That is, they can benefit from the 'diversity dividend'.

Structure and Responsibility

Closely linked to clarity of direction is clarity of structure and responsibility. It is essential that team members know who is responsible for specific goals and actions. This particularly relates to team composition; there should be clear reason for each team member to have a place on the team, and they should each have clear responsibility for activities that contribute to the mission, strategy, etc.

Again, this may seem obvious, and many team members will tell you when asked that their structure and responsibilities are clear. However, I have seen – particularly in organisations which pride themselves on being fast paced – enormous amounts of costly, duplicated effort and infighting due to different people believing they are responsible for the same goal. This is largely because it isn't clear who is responsible for what, and assumptions are made about ownership of goals. Sometimes we see the opposite – things fall between the cracks and don't get done, because everyone assumes someone else is doing it (otherwise known as the bystander effect).

In my many years of running team development workshops, I have found that teams typically enjoy building relationships, discussing challenges and solving problems, but when we come to the question of exactly what action is going to be taken and by whom, the energy drops, and it can be like pulling teeth getting the team to discuss and make a decision. As a team development facilitator, you have to become comfortable with taking the team out of their comfort zone to help them create clear actions and assign actions to the right owners. And as a high performing team, you have to learn to take ownership yourselves of creating clarity of structure and responsibility. This is not a once and done exercise. You should do it every time a decision is made.

Some people take advantage of ambiguity of accountability to 'socially loaf', which is when an individual puts in less effort because they know others will pick up the slack. This is one reason some leaders struggle with the concept of team goals or account-ability: they fear it will allow some people to hide in the crowd and get the benefits of others' hard work. According to social psycholo-gist Donelson Forsyth, there are several ways to reduce the likeli-hood of social loafing – and they are strongly aligned with the behaviours in the Accountability sub-cluster (see below). The first is to establish individual accountability, the second is to assign clear responsibilities and the third is to encourage team loyalty.

I would suggest that the individual accountability Forsyth identi-fies is *not* instead of the shared accountability we discuss in the next section. It is possible to feel accountable for group goals *and* to understand our specific individual role in achieving those outcomes, and therefore feel responsible for the individual element too. It is both rather than either/or.

SUB-CLUSTER: ACCOUNTABILITY

Diane Arias describes the essence of Accountability: 'Team spirit is knowing and living the belief that what a group of people can accomplish together is much larger, far greater and will exceed that which an individual can accomplish alone.'

This mindset enables team members to feel responsible for the team performance, not just for meeting their individual goals. Therefore, they collaborate, focus on team process (see Growth chapter) as well as performance, and feel able to hold each other accountable for achieving team and individual goals.

This is partly achieved by involving the team in the development of the strategy and plans so they feel shared ownership. It is closely linked to the Direction element of this cluster, in that the team first need to have a shared direction and goals that they feel jointly accountable for achieving.

The Five Cs

The Five Cs model helpfully describes a range of ways teams can work together. It is an evolution of the Four Cs model as I have added *competition* to recognise the role that competition between team members can play in team behaviours.

Collaboration is an interesting word and is often used interchangeably with terms such as *coordination* and *cooperation*. They are, however, distinct and important aspects of teamwork. Many teams will describe themselves as collaborating when in fact they are cooperating or coordinating.

I have outlined the difference between the terms below to form a helpful framework for evaluating team meetings. It can help you understand the purpose of your meetings and ensure they don't default to simply being a method for communication, which (particularly in these technology-enabled times) can easily be achieved in less time consuming ways.

You will notice the model also includes *competition*. We sometimes see team members withholding information and resources so that they can 'win'. Indeed, some leaders believe that competition between team members is a good way to motivate them to work hard. I do not subscribe to this idea. If a team genuinely has shared goals, creating competition between team members will encourage unhelpful behaviours that work towards individual rather than shared goals.

The Five Cs

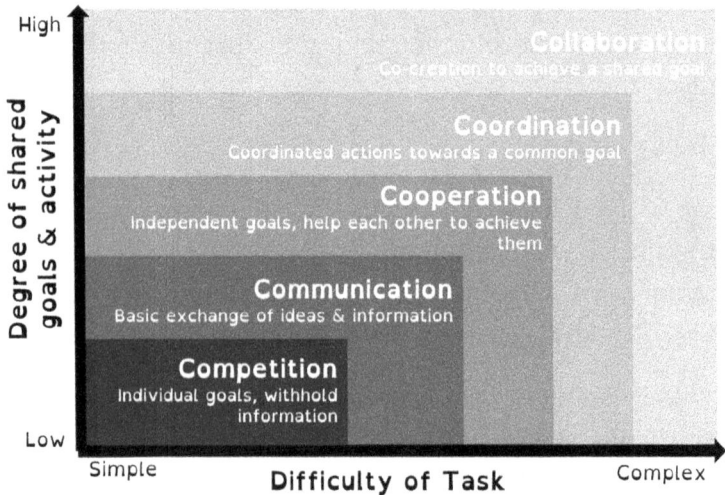

Collaboration
Co-creation to achieve a shared goal

Coordination
Coordinated actions towards a common goal

Cooperation
Independent goals, help each other to achieve them

Communication
Basic exchange of ideas & information

Competition
Individual goals, withhold information

Degree of shared goals & activity: High — Low
Difficulty of Task: Simple — Complex

To illustrate the five Cs in a team setting:

Competition

Team members compete to achieve their individual goals faster or better than other team members. They may try to block other team members' progress. I have often seen this in teams with very ambitious or financially motivated individuals who see other team members as competition for their next promotion or bonus.

Communication

Team members update each other about their individual activities/progress towards their individual goals. The aim is to keep others informed. My observation is that this takes up the vast majority of time in team meetings. In most cases it could have been communicated in another way.

Cooperation

Team members support each other to achieve their individual goals by sharing information, responding quickly to requests, and sharing resources, for example, and by not getting in each other's way. They do not need to be aware of each other's goals.

Coordination

Team members work together to achieve a shared goal. The work is coordinated, and individual tasks are assigned. For example, sales and marketing will coordinate their efforts around a new product launch. They each have their individual tasks, but they have a shared plan to ensure everything happens at the right time so that others can complete their tasks.

Collaboration

Team members have a shared vision of the goals and work together to create something they could not have created independently.

Collaboration is about creating something new that relies on the combined expertise of the people involved.

For example, in an HR team, the Heads of DEI, L&D and Recruitment work together to develop an Inclusive Recruitment programme to be rolled out to all Hiring Managers. They collectively agree the goals and outcomes, brainstorm solutions together and work together (not separately) to create a new programme that combines DEI, Learning and Development, and Recruitment expertise. The outcome is something none of them could have produced alone.

Many teams spend a disproportionate amount of time communicating, and very little genuinely collaborating. Often when people think they are collaborating they are actually coordinating – they are aligning their efforts but are missing the magic that comes from co-creation. It is only through collaboration that we access the team's collective intelligence (see Adaptability chapter for more on this).

We do not need to collaborate all of the time, but it is essential when it comes to solving complex problems without an obvious answer, and where a diverse range of perspectives and experiences are invaluable in creating a solution. Senior teams in particular can find it difficult to collaborate, in part because the individual team members have typically achieved success and been consistently rewarded for their individual efforts. When they are placed in a situation where collaboration is needed, they have not practised the required skills, and may not have the collaborative mindset. This links back to the need for shared goals and team purpose: the team members need to believe they are accountable for shared goals as well as individual ones.

Shared Accountability

I first came across the concept of shared accountability when reading *The Wisdom of Teams* by Katzenbach and Smith, which is considered a classic read for those interested in team performance.

They advocate that a team's performance includes both individual results and 'collective work products' that two or more members work on together. This means the team requires both individual and group goals and accountability.

When teams describe themselves as 'siloed' this indicates that they operate independently and focus on individual rather than team accountabilities.

Applying the topics covered in this chapter will contribute to generating shared accountability in the team, but there are additional elements that will also help. These include:

- Building trust and an ability to hold difficult conversations (see Trust chapter), particularly if the team are to hold each other accountable rather than believing it is the responsibility of the team leader.
- Goals that link to the team purpose with regular monitoring and feedback against the goals (see Growth chapter for more on goals and the 'zone of optimal performance'). This helps keep the team on track and feeling accountable.
- Reward mechanisms that recognise team as well as individual performance. It is important to reward and recognise all the behaviours that contribute towards creating an inclusive high performing team. This helps reinforce the behaviours and is a mechanism to encourage team members to change. Note that reward does not have

to be financial. Praise and recognition are equally important.

Everyday Actions to Build Alignment in Your Team – for Team Members

- Work with other team members to develop your team's shared vision, purpose, identity, goals and plans.
- Help create clarity of team structure, roles and responsibilities.
- Support the creation of a team identity and share your pride at being part of the team with team members and others outside the team.
- Ensure you understand how your individual goals align with the team's goals/purpose etc.
- Keep your conflicts and disagreements within the team – don't air your dirty laundry in public!
- Find ways to connect the team's purpose to your own individual purpose.
- Ensure that you feel accountable for your own performance and the performance of the team – allow others to hold you accountable.
- Hold other team members accountable for their individual and the team's performance.
- Analyse how much time the team spends on each of the Five Cs. Work towards increasing collaboration with other team members where it would add value.
- Put up your hand and offer to take on responsibility for tasks that benefit the team as a whole.
- Help new team members quickly understand the team purpose, goals, structure, etc., so that they can be aligned.

Everyday Actions to Build Alignment in Your Team – for Team Leaders

- Invest time in co-creation of alignment with the team – don't jump straight to activity.
- Involve the team in developing a shared vision, purpose, identity, goals and plans.
- Link the team vision, strategy, purpose, etc., to the organisational strategy and vision.
- Work with the team to create clarity of team structure, roles and responsibilities. The RACI model can be a useful tool to help do this.
- Regularly review the team structure, roles and responsibilities to ensure they are still relevant, and that new team members are aligned.
- Monitor and give regular feedback on performance, not just at the end of a project/year.
- Work to create a team identity and share your pride at being part of the team with team members and others outside the team.
- Give space for resolving conflicts and disagreements within the team – don't allow them to air the team's dirty laundry in public!
- Work on your own individual purpose and share with the team how that connects to the team's purpose.
- Hold team members accountable for both individual and team performance. Don't allow individual superstars to damage the team dynamic just because they have high levels of individual performance.
- Encourage the team members to hold each other accountable for their individual and team performance.

- Spend time analysing the Five Cs and encourage increased collaboration in the team. There is an exercise at the end of this chapter that will help with this.

Two Questions to Measure Alignment in Your Team

You can ask your team members to score the team using two questions. Ask them to give scores from one (Never) to five (Always).

1. Are the team aligned around the team vision, strategy and purpose?
2. Do the team feel shared accountability for achieving the team vision, strategy and purpose?

Team Development Exercises to Develop Alignment in Your Team

Here are two exercises you can use with your team to develop the Alignment cluster. The first is for Direction and the second is for Accountability. You can facilitate them yourself or ask a member of the team to do it. See Chapter Six for further information about facilitating team exercises.

Alignment Cluster: Direction Exercise

'Purpose' Activity

The aim of this exercise is to develop a purpose statement your team can align around. It serves as your 'north star' – a motivating vision of what you can achieve as a team that is different from your goals and targets and gives the team members something to emotionally connect with. You can use it to:

- Make and explain team decisions.
- Give context in meetings and presentations.
- Help decide where the team spends their time and energy.

This exercise also develops behaviours in other clusters such as Growth (focusing on the way the team works together) and Adaptability (building on each other's ideas).

You can download this exercise and the team member handout via the Liberare Consulting website – a link can be found at the back of the book.

Team Pre-work – estimated time 30 minutes:

1. Share the 'Purpose' handout with the team and ask them to complete it in advance of the session.
2. Ensure the team know that they will be discussing the pre-work in the team session, so it is important that they do complete it beforehand and bring it to the session with them.

Facilitator Pre-work – estimated time 60 minutes:

1. Complete the handout yourself so you can share your thoughts in the workshop, but also so you can answer the team's questions when they are filling it out.
2. Re-read the chapter on Alignment to remind yourself why you are doing this exercise, and to identify the key messages you want to share with the team.

At the Team Session – 5 minutes intro, 20 minutes activity, 25 minutes debrief

Introduce the reason for the activity (5 minutes)

This activity is designed to help your team agree their team purpose. Purpose is the motivation and source of meaning that drives people to do their best work. A team purpose is the north star; it guides our behaviour and gives us something to follow and evaluate decisions against.

Remind them and get their agreement to confidentiality. What is discussed in the room stays in the room. They can share their personal story and experience outside the room, but they should not share anything that anyone else has said or done.

Start the activity (20 minutes)

Split the team into groups of three or four. This is quite a short time allowance for the for the small group activity, so they will need to work quickly. This is to ensure there is plenty of time for the larger group discussion. If you have longer than fifty minutes allocated to the exercise, you could give more time to this part of the activity.

Explain that they have three tasks in their small groups:

1. Quickly share their responses to the pre-work questions: no more than a couple of minutes per person.
2. Identify key themes for each of the four topics (Stakeholders, Goals, Values, Purpose) that were shared across the group.
3. Ask them to nominate a spokesperson to share back key themes.

Whilst the team hold their small group discussions, get four flip charts and write the four headings from the pre-work sheet at the tops of them: Flipchart 1 'Stakeholders'; Flipchart 2 'Goals';

Flipchart 3 'Values'; Flipchart 4 'Purpose'. Attach the flipcharts to the wall.

Note that as the facilitator, you do not go into any of the small groups. You can wander around and check in to see if they have any questions, but do not get drawn into a long conversation with any group.

Debrief as a group (25 minutes)

Get each group to share the key themes from their discussions. Start with Stakeholders and ask for a comment from each group, then move to Goals and ask each group, then repeat for Values and Purpose. This keeps it a bit more interesting as you are hearing from different groups all the time. Write the themes up on the four different flipcharts.

Ask the team to look at the Purpose flipchart and think of Purpose statements that capture the key themes from all the groups. Remember that you are trying to capture why you uniquely exist as a team.

You might find the following structure useful, but don't feel constrained if it doesn't work for you:

Our Team
what we do   to/for   audience

so that
                              impact

Don't worry about wordsmithing at this stage, just try to get down some key words and phrases that resonate with the team.

It is possible you won't finish the exercise in the time you have available. That will partly depend on how aligned the team is already. You may find a lot of variation in the answers you get to the first three topics (Stakeholders, Goals and Values) in which case it makes sense to spend time discussing those topics and getting greater alignment before you move on to the team Purpose.

If you don't finish you can either revisit the topic later or get a small group of volunteers to work on the purpose statement and bring it back to the team at a later date. Make sure you agree on who is going to do it and when they are going to report back so that it doesn't get forgotten. You can use the GARU model to help you plan:

- Goal – what have you decided needs to be done? What is your goal?
- Action – what action(s) need to take place in order to achieve this.
- Responsibility – who is going to take responsibility for making it happen? Who else will be involved?
- Update – when will they report back on their progress to the wider team?

Keep the Momentum Going

When you have an agreed purpose statement, make sure it isn't put in a drawer and forgotten. Put it up on the wall, include it in your PowerPoint presentations, be creative about where you put it so the team can see it regularly and it can become a living thing that helps you make decisions, align and remind you why the team's work is important.

Review the purpose statement from time to time to ensure it is still relevant and to make sure new team members understand where it came from and why it is important to the team.

ALIGNMENT CLUSTER: ACCOUNTABILITY EXERCISE

'Collaboration' Activity

The purpose of this exercise is to use the Five Cs model to explore team collaboration behaviours.

It also develops behaviours in other clusters such as Growth (focus on continuous improvement) and Adaptability (focus on innovation).

You can download this exercise and the team member handout via the Liberare Consulting website – a link can be found at the back of the book.

Team Pre-work – estimated time 30 minutes:

1. Share the 'Collaboration Exercise' handout with the team and ask them to complete it in advance of the session.
2. Ensure the team know they will be discussing the pre-work in the team session, so it is important they complete it beforehand and bring it to the session with them.

Facilitator Pre-work – estimated time 60 minutes:

1. Complete the handout yourself so you can share your thoughts in the workshop, but also so you can answer the team's questions when they are filling it out.
2. Re-read the chapter on Alignment to remind yourself why you are doing this exercise, and to identify the key messages you want to share with the team.

At the Team Session – 5 minutes intro, 25 minutes activity, 20 minutes debrief

Introduce the reason for the activity (5 minutes)

Begin with an explanation of *collaboration*. For example: The more complex and challenging a task, the more a team needs to collaborate in order to get a great result. Often, we think we are collaborating when actually we are simply cooperating or coordinating our activity. True collaboration requires us to have a shared goal and to work together to achieve that goal.

Remind them about and get their agreement to confidentiality. What is discussed in the room stays in the room. They can share their personal story and experience outside the room, but they should not share anything that anyone else has said or done.

Start the activity (25 minutes)

Split the team into groups of around four people.

Give them instructions for the small group activity:

1. Each team member is to share what they have written in their pre-work.
2. Identify and discuss any themes that emerged from what they have shared.
3. Nominate a spokesperson to share the key themes with the larger group.

Check to see if there are any questions, and then get them to start the task.

As the facilitator, you do not go into any of the small groups. You can wander around and check in to see if they have any questions, but do not get drawn into a long conversation with any group.

Debrief as a group (20 minutes)

Get each small group to share back their key themes.

Facilitate a discussion with the whole group. You could use these questions:

- Were there any themes you heard repeated across the groups?
- What does this tell us about how we behave as a team?
- How can we incorporate this learning to make our team more inclusive (as individuals and collectively)?
- What actions do we need to take and by when?
- Who is going to own that?
- Is there anything you'd like to see me do differently (if you are the team leader) to help with this?
- What are you individually going to do differently?

Keep the Momentum Going

A typical outcome of this exercise is that the team identify they are not collaborating enough, and they could achieve better outcomes if they tried to do this more.

Sometimes this conversation leads on to one about team meetings and the purpose of the meetings. One team I worked with completely re-worked their meeting cadence and agendas to create more time for important conversations during their meetings (not just communicating updates).

It is important to keep this conversation live and to keep revisiting the amount of collaboration happening in the team to ensure that the commitments and decisions made during this exercise are not forgotten.

REFERENCES

Disciplined Collaboration: 4 steps to collaborative success (Emmanuel Gobillot, 2021) - https://amzn.to/45HutYq

How to live to be 100+ (Dan Buettner, 2009) - https://www.ted.com/talks/dan_buettner_how_to_live_to_be_100

Purpose is Everything: How brands that authentically lead with purpose are changing the nature of business today (Deloitte, 2019) - https://www2.deloitte.com/us/en/insights/topics/marketing-and-sales-operations/global-marketing-trends/2020/purpose-driven-companies.html

Purpose in Life and Its Relationship to All-Cause Mortality and Cardiovascular Events: A Meta-Analysis (Cohen, Bavishi & Rozanski, 2015) - https://www.researchgate.net/publication/285585398_Purpose_in_Life_and_Its_Relationship_to_All-Cause_Mortality_and_Cardiovascular_Events_A_Meta-Analysis

Self-Categorization With a Novel Mixed-Race Group Moderates Automatic Social and Racial Biases (Van Bavel & Cunningham, 2008) - https://www.researchgate.net/publication/23679809_Self-Categorization_With_a_Novel_Mixed-Race_Group_Moderates_Automatic_Social_and_Racial_Biases

Teaming Up or Down? A Multisource Study on the Role of Team Identification and Learning in the Team Diversity–Performance Link (Van veelen & Ufkes, 2017) - https://www.researchgate.net/publication/322164052_Teaming_Up_or_Down_A_Multisource_Study_on_the_Role_of_Team_Identification_and_Learning_in_the_Team_Diversity-Performance_Link

Teamwork at the top (McKinsey Quarterly, 2001) - https://www.mckinsey.com/capabilities/people-and-organizational-performance/our-insights/teamwork-at-the-top

The Discipline of Teams (Katzenbach & Smith, 1993) - https://hbr.org/1993/03/the-discipline-of-teams-2

The Wisdom of Teams: Creating the High-Performance Organization (Katzenbach & Smith, 2015) - https://amzn.to/3M9TSmO

To Affinity And Beyond: From Me to We, The Rise of The Purpose-Led Brand (Accenture, 2018) - https://www.accenture.com/_acnmedia/thought-leadership-assets/pdf/accenture-competitiveagility-gcpr-pov.pdf

Chapter 3

Growth

"Our destiny is not written for us, it is written by us."

— *Barack Obama*

Why Is Growth Important?

If a team is to respond to the rapid and constant fluctuations of the VUCA world where 'change is the only constant in life' (Heraclitus, 500BC), it is essential to focus on learning, continuous improvement and growth – both of the team members and the team itself.

From an engagement and retention perspective, there are also good reasons to provide growth opportunities to team members. Both Gallup and Korn Ferry indicate that development or growth opportunities are in the top five drivers of employee engagement. Culture Amp found that development is the number one driver of engagement for millennials – they state that people who felt they had access to the learning and development they needed were 21 percent more engaged than those who didn't.

A 2019 LinkedIn Workforce Learning Report found that 94 percent of employees would stay at a company longer if the company invested in their career development. The research found that roughly a quarter of Gen Z and Millennials say learning is the number one thing that makes them happy at work, and 27 percent of Gen Z and Millennials say the number one reason they'd leave their job is because they did not have the opportunity to learn and grow. Millennials (born between 1981 and 1996) are currently the largest segment of employees in the workplace. Gen Z (born between 1997 and 2012) are the largest generation overall in the population and are hot on Millennials' heels in the workplace.

In our model there are two aspects to Growth: Development and Improvement. Development has a more individual focus. The emphasis is placed on the importance of development for all, and the level of comfort with feedback, recognition and praise in the team. Improvement is important at a team *and* individual level, and places importance on continuous improvement, learning from mistakes, goal setting and creating an environment where team members can work in their zone of optimal performance.

Sub-cluster: Development

This sub-cluster explores how to make development available and important to everyone in the team, and the role of feedback in supporting development.

Development for All

In an inclusive high performing team, development opportunities and time for development are available to all, not just those judged as 'point people' or high potentials. I mentioned this concept of 'point people' in the chapter on Trust. It is one of the diversity challenges we frequently see in organisations in that team leaders have certain team members they rely on more than others, and it is those people who tend to get the stretch assignments and development opportunities such as training and coaching.

This creates a virtuous spiral for the 'point people' who have opportunities to impress and continue to develop their skills and build their experiences. In addition, we tend to give 'point people' more slack – we give them more support and they can make a mistake without too many consequences.

Everyone else experiences a vicious cycle of not getting opportunities and therefore they don't get the chance to build trust and confidence in their performance. They don't get the opportunity to develop skills that will help them in their current and future roles. For people who are not our 'point people' we may offer less support and have less tolerance for mistakes.

Often, we focus on the role of the team leader when it comes to providing growth and development opportunities for the team. However, I believe it is the responsibility of the whole team to look out for each other. For example, one team member may have a project that would be developmental for someone else in the team to get involved in. Or perhaps they recognise that they always get certain opportunities and can step aside to allow someone else in the team to get the experience.

I heard Katherine Ryan (a UK based Canadian comedian) give a good example of this on the High Performance podcast. She recognised that the UK TV comedy scene is still very biased towards men, and that there was rarely more than one woman invited onto the weekly panel show *Mock the Week*. The show is well known and a great springboard for up-and-coming comedians. She had already become reasonably famous and took the decision to refuse the frequent invitations she received to appear on the show, as she knew other less well-known female comedians would then be invited and get an opportunity to appear. She recognised her role in creating opportunities for other women, even though she was not in a leadership position.

Relying on 'point people' feels easy for an individual. It doesn't feel like a risk and may feel like less time is required by the team member because they believe that they can just trust the person to get on with it. Choosing someone who is not a 'point person' for a stretch assignment or development opportunity feels much riskier. They are less confident that the task will be performed well and may feel they need to stay more closely involved.

Research suggests us that our 'point people' tend to be those who are most like us, which creates a danger that our under-represented colleagues do not get the same opportunities. This contributes to them not developing at the same rate and may contribute to slower progression through the organisation.

In hybrid teams, there is also the potential to show proximity bias and offer development opportunities to people we see more regularly, as it can be easy to forget people who are in the office less often. I learnt this the hard way in my early days as a consultant. I was often travelling or on clients' sites, and I noticed that people who were more regularly in the office tended to get involved in some of the interesting work that I would have enjoyed, simply because they were physically around when decisions were being made.

In an inclusive high performing team, consideration is given to the development of all team members. Everybody is given growth and development opportunities, and they are all expected to spend time and energy focusing on their own and each other's personal development. This means the team need to take risks on people they perhaps don't know so well or who are different from themselves.

I really recognise this feeling of risk from my days working in a very busy global consultancy. As a senior member of the consultancy team, I was responsible for multiple client projects that ran concurrently. I typically took the Client Relationship Director role, which meant that I delegated the day-to-day running of the projects to various colleagues.

Stakes were high, and clients rightly had elevated expectations: they were paying a lot of money, and the projects were often high profile. The pressure and fear of failure drove a strong temptation to try to get my trusted colleagues or 'point people' to be part of my project team. As the author of a book called *The Inclusive Team*, I am aware of the irony that my behaviour really wasn't inclusive at all! Sometimes, life has a way of teaching you a lesson, and I was forced to overcome my fears when my favourite project manager left the business, and I had to rely on the resourcing team to find me a replacement.

Even though I have now left that role, I still remember the anxiety of being allocated someone completely unknown to me and new to the business into a pivotal role in the project team. It felt like a real personal risk, but also one I had no choice but to take.

I also remember the absolute joy of finding that the person allocated to me was a complete superstar who enormously surpassed my expectations and has since gone on to much bigger and better things. This was a great lesson in managing my own anxiety and risk appetite. Giving someone an opportunity was (a) more inclusive, and (b) had a positive impact on both them and me.

Feedback

Feedback, recognition and praise are closely linked to development, as they help us know how we are perceived to be performing. They can help us learn faster, reach higher skill levels quicker, and can ensure our work is aligned with that of other team members. Netflix founder Reed Hastings suggests in his book *No Rules Rules* that candid feedback is one of the top three ingredients of an innovative organisation.

However, despite Ken Blanchard's suggestion that, "Feedback is the breakfast of champions," and Warren Buffet telling us that, "Feedback is a gift," I have found that teams are often uncomfortable with it.

Research by Quantum Workplace supports this. They found that just over half of respondents want to receive more recognition from their immediate manager or supervisor, and 41 percent want to receive more recognition from immediate colleagues. A 2019 survey by Zenger Folkman found that 94 percent of respondents said corrective feedback improved their performance when it was presented well, with two-thirds saying their performance and possibilities for success would have increased if they had been given more feedback.

The picture becomes increasingly complicated in diverse teams. Research in 2022 and 2023 by Textio found differences in the amount, quality and type of feedback received by different demographic groups. For example, women received more feedback about their personality (rather than their behaviours) than men. Asian people received the most feedback, with Black employees getting more unactionable feedback and Black men receiving the least feedback overall. Non-binary, transgender and gender non-conforming people report receiving insufficient feedback 1.5 times more than men.

There are also different expectations and understandings about what constructive feedback looks like. A recent article in the Harvard Business Review (see references) captured some of these differences from the perspective of nationality, gender and age. For example, feedback that is considered clear and helpful in one culture may be considered overly direct in another.

In addition to these challenges, several elements contribute to a team's struggle with feedback:

Feedback Is Threatening

People associate feedback with criticism rather than recognition or praise, and it is often limited to annual or twice-yearly appraisal conversations rather than being routinely requested and given. In addition, unsolicited feedback tends to feel like an unwanted gift.

Research suggests that both the feedback giver and the feedback receiver are uncomfortable with feedback. Studies show some people experience an increased heartrate equivalent to the level of someone giving a public presentation (which many people find one of the most anxiety inducing things they can do). I outlined in the introduction how our brains respond to perceived threat (both physical and social) and receiving unsolicited feedback, particularly negative feedback, is perceived by our brains as a threat to social aspects such as our status and self-image/ego. This means the feedback (even if accurate and well-intended) is likely to put our brains into a state that isn't conducive to growth.

Sheila Heen and Douglas Stone write in the Harvard Business Review that there are three triggers that can get activated when receiving negative feedback:

- Truth triggers – when the feedback feels wrong or unhelpful.

- Relationship triggers – which are influenced by your relationship with the person giving feedback (e.g., do you respect them?).
- Identity triggers – when the feedback challenges your self-image of who you are. This can be particularly strong if you (often unconsciously) feel insecure about something, and a piece of feedback relates to that insecurity.

It can be helpful to think of feedback you have received in the past and identify if any of these triggers were true for you. I can think of one piece of feedback I received early in my consulting career after facilitating a workshop. The feedback was that they found my hair distracting. I have long, slightly wild hair, and a habit of playing with it, particularly when nervous. I actually found the feedback helpful as I could see that it might be annoying to programme participants. I think it was easy to take because it didn't trigger me in any of the three ways listed above.

In contrast, around the same time, I received some feedback from my manager that she thought I still dressed like a student. I was thirty years old at the time, and I think it triggered me in two of the ways Heen and Stone identify. Firstly, I didn't rate the dress sense of my manager, so I didn't respect their judgement, and secondly, it was a threat to my self-image. It may have been accurate, but I wasn't ready to hear it.

Interestingly, I took notice of the first feedback and started wearing my hair tied up when facilitating. I ignored the second piece of feedback and continued dressing the same way.

Previous Negative Experiences

There are also challenges associated with previous experiences in giving and receiving feedback. Team members expect the situation to be the same as their previous experience.

If team members have previously given feedback to individuals or the organisation, but have seen little change, there may be some learned helplessness around giving feedback: they have learned that it has little impact and don't bother speaking up anymore. A more extreme case could be that team members have given feedback, and it has been received badly, again resulting in a reluctance to do it.

They may have also had a negative experience with receiving feedback in the past. Perhaps it was poorly worded or felt unfair (see the 'truth trigger' above), which led to a reluctance to ask for others' views.

For example, a podcast guest of mine spoke about feedback she received as a young woman in the early days of her career referring to her blonde hair and the pitch of her voice. It felt unfair as she couldn't do much about it, but it had a long-lasting effect on her self-confidence (see the link in the references to listen to this episode).

Feedback Habits

My experience from supporting leaders to interpret their 360-degree feedback reports is that they tend to go one of two ways – they either defend their self-image by rejecting any negative feedback, or they believe the feedback is completely true rather than just somebody else's perspective and it damages their self-esteem (sometimes permanently).

Interestingly, I find the same with praise – some people find it very difficult to hear and really take on praise; they instantly focus on the negative, even if it is just five percent of the overall feedback. Positive feedback and praise are an incredibly important aspect of helping us feel valued for our contribution and for keeping us on the right track. Team leaders and members need to make their feedback positive as well as negative. The receivers of praise need to listen to and absorb the positive messages from others.

Feedback can be incredibly helpful if individuals are in the right mindset to receive it – that is, when it isn't perceived as threatening but as useful information to help accelerate growth and development. It is a core element of a growth mindset, which you can read more about later in this chapter.

It is important to remember that feedback isn't the truth, it is simply somebody else's perspective as seen through their eyes. Whilst it can be very helpful to understand their perspective, it doesn't mean you have to do anything with the feedback. Somebody once gave me a quote – it may be a Chinese proverb – that I think gives a helpful perspective on feedback:

"If one man calls you an ass, ignore him. If two men call you an ass, start looking for tracks. If three men call you an ass, put on a harness."

An isolated piece of feedback carries less weight than if you receive the same feedback from multiple sources.

How to improve the feedback culture in the team

There are several ways that teams can overcome the feedback challenges outlined in this chapter. In the spirit of inclusion, I would encourage you to work with the team to understand individual preferences around feedback and collectively agree actions that will build a team feedback culture. The exercise at the end of this chapter will give you an opportunity to do that.

Build feedback into the day to day. Don't save feedback as a once-a-year formal activity. Build feedback loops into regular team activities. For example, build in project reviews to explore what went well and what could have gone better, or develop the habit of a quick debrief after meetings. The more you normalise ad-hoc feedback the easier it becomes to both give and receive. You may find using a specific format (e.g. Stop, Start, Continue) helpful so that everyone gives feedback following the same format.

Encourage asking for feedback. This relates to the point above. If you create a culture where giving and receiving feedback is normalised, you can also create a culture where people ask for feedback rather than waiting for it to be given. See the section below for further detail on this.

Balance of praise and constructive feedback. We often associate feedback with negative criticism, but praise and recognition are equally important. We need to know what we are doing well as well as what we could do better. I have worked for managers whose way of giving praise was an absence of criticism. I would have preferred some direct praise too!

Ask the team. Find out from each individual how they feel about feedback: how and when they like to receive it; what their triggers are; what positive and negative feedback experiences they have had in the past.

Ensure equity in feedback. Under-represented groups tend to get less feedback overall and less actionable feedback. Reflect on the feedback you give to ensure you are not avoiding giving feedback to any individuals.

Focus on behaviours and impact. Unhelpful feedback is often vague, emotionally laden, and is sometimes focused on the person not the behaviour. It doesn't give the receiver much information about what they specifically did. In contrast, helpful feedback tends to be specific, about behaviours and helps the receiver understand the impact the behaviour had. *Situation, Behaviour, Impact* (SBI) is a useful acronym to remember.

For example, helpful feedback might sound like: 'When you presented to the client on Monday, you did a great job of preparing a succinct and professional looking slide deck and answering all their questions calmly and correctly.' Unhelpful feedback might sound like: 'Great job with the client on Monday.'

There is an exercise at the end of this chapter that gives your team an opportunity to practise giving each other feedback.

How to receive feedback

I always try to help my clients understand the impact of the behaviour they have received feedback on. For instance, you may have received feedback that (i) you do not demonstrate strategic thinking and (ii) you do not always provide as much clarity as possible. If your job does not require you to be strategic, but it does require you to delegate, you may want to focus on developing clarity above strategic thinking. However, if your longer-term aspiration is to move into a senior leadership role, you may want to focus on the strategic thinking feedback as well.

If we are in the right mindset for feedback we are more likely to be able to maintain some sense of perspective and see it as information we can choose to use or discard, rather than an attack on our self-image.

The key is to remain curious and not immediately accept or deny the feedback. I personally find this quite difficult, particularly when the feedback is positive and given spontaneously. I feel embarrassed and try to move too quickly to change the subject. Only afterwards do I wish I had shown more curiosity as often I would like more specifics than the general feedback that was given. I am trying to learn to manage myself and engage my curiosity in the moment.

The NeuroLeadership Institute suggests that asking for feedback has a more positive effect than it being imposed on an individual. This seems to offer both the receiver and the giver much more psychological safety than a giver-led approach and means that the feedback recipient is likely to be more open and less defensive.

They find that:

- Both sides feel less threatened: the 'asker' feels more in control, and the 'giver' is clear about what is wanted.
- You get feedback more quickly and regularly which allows you to course correct more rapidly.
- You can ask many people, giving you a broader range of perspectives.
- You get the specific feedback you need and want.

SUB-CLUSTER: IMPROVEMENT

The improvement sub-cluster brings together several factors that influence a team's collective and individual growth and improvement in performance. The first factor is a collective striving for continuous improvement which includes team process improvement. The second is our response to goals and how we get into the zone of optimal performance. The final factor is our attitude to growth – or our growth mindset.

Continuous Improvement

McKinsey describes this as '...an ongoing effort to improve all elements of an organization. It rests on the belief that a steady stream of improvements, diligently executed, will have transformational results.' It suggests that team members don't want to stand still and that they want to steadily improve their own and the team's performance, with goals being set that reflect that desire.

Continuous improvement differs from innovation in that it is a steady focus on small improvements of things that already exist. Innovation is the creation of something new and tends to be more radical. Both are important, and we explore team innovation in the Adaptability chapter.

A range of project management philosophies have continuous improvement as a foundational concept, such as lean, total quality management, agile and six sigma. Your organisation may favour one of these and provide helpful resources and guidance for their application. There are useful techniques that can be used in any team to help cultivate a continuous improvement mindset:

Without Blame Retrospectives. Review projects/initiatives to explore what went well and what could have been done better. Alternatively, you can hold regular scheduled retrospective meetings that cover a range of topics and are not linked to any specific project or initiative. An important element of the retrospective is that you do not look for someone to blame – mistakes are an opportunity for learning not punishment. This helps create trust, psychological safety and a growth mindset in the team.

Five Whys. Also known as root cause analysis, this simple technique requires the continuous asking of 'why' to uncover the underlying causes of something rather than the symptoms. Note that you don't need to stop at five whys. You can keep on asking until you get to an actionable root cause. For example:

Problem... *Our website traffic has reduced.*

- Why? Fewer people are being exposed to our site.
- Why? Fewer people are seeing our digital advertising.
- Why? The ad campaign is no longer running on Facebook.
- Why? Our company account is past due.

- Why? The company credit card linked to Facebook has expired.
- Why? The person whose card it was has left the company.
- Why? There is no master list of services linked to individual credit cards.

Outcome... the team creates an action to make a list of services that are set up for automatic payments with company credit cards.

PDCA. This stands for Plan-Do-Check-Act and is a widely known and used tool. The first three actions (Plan, Do, Check) are implemented on a small scale to allow for testing and revising with a small group of users/customers before the broader roll out (Act).

Ten Principles of Kaisen. This is not an activity but a useful set of principles that support a continuous improvement mindset. You may have seen them expressed slightly differently, but the underlying message remains the same:

- Let go of assumptions; accept no excuses.
- Be proactive about solving problems – if something is wrong, correct it.
- Don't accept the status quo.
- Let go of perfectionism and take an attitude of iterative, adaptive change.
- Look for solutions (not blame) as you find mistakes – improve everything continuously.
- Create an environment in which everyone feels empowered to contribute (see Trust chapter).
- Don't accept the obvious issue; instead, ask 'why' five times to get to the root cause (see above).
- Get information and opinions from multiple people (see Inclusive Design section in the Adaptability chapter).

- Use creativity to find low-cost, small improvements and reinvest on further improvements.
- Never stop improving.

Team Process Improvement

A key factor in building an inclusive high performing team is to pay attention to team dynamics and processes as well as to achieving goals. It is very common for teams to focus purely on the task. Conversations and meetings revolve around achieving the task and very little, if any, attention is given to the relationships and processes that help the team perform at their best.

So many teams I have worked with have focused on task, task, task and ignored some quite important interpersonal dynamics and behavioural issues. This has resulted in burnout and high turnover. They then turn to someone like me to help them with the team, but by that point it is a long and challenging road to get the team back to equilibrium.

Perhaps we do this because human beings are messy and complex, and it seems easier to ignore this and focus on things we believe are more controllable – such as team tasks and goals. However, we ignore team dynamics at our peril. We are not just resources or machines that turn up, do a job and go home; we bring our experiences, our intellect, our motivations and our social needs to work.

A team is also not a static entity: team members will leave, others will join, organisations will be restructured, and teams will be split and combined with other teams. Therefore, teams will inevitably be complex, dynamic systems which will perform sub-optimally if we don't regularly give focus to the interaction between members.

High performing teams spend time improving how they work as a team – not just once a year at an away day, but on a regular basis so they continue to develop their levels of Trust, Alignment, Growth, Adaptability and Respect.

I wrote this book as a guide for team leaders, team members and those who work with teams. It is an aid to team process improvement which helps you understand the elements that make up an inclusive high performing team. It is also a resource to help you work with your team(s) to develop these behaviours.

The ten-question survey (one of the downloads that accompanies this book) allows you to diagnose areas of strength and areas to develop. The bullet lists at the end of each chapter in this book are checklists for team leaders and team members to take responsibility for developing the team on a day-to-day basis. The exercises are intended to help you work with your team(s) to surface thoughts, ideas and challenges and to strengthen how you work together.

Zone of Optimal Performance

This relates to the setting of individual and team goals that allow the team to continue to stretch and grow. A mistake that is commonly made is to set incredibly stretching goals that are impossible to reach. I have observed a lot of goal setting based on wishes and aspiration rather than data and an understanding of human motivation.

I have seen leaders implement a twenty percent financial growth target for all revenue generating departments and countries, regardless of their particular circumstances or economy. I have seen mandated fifteen percent headcount reductions applied to all departments with no consideration given to workload. Not to mention million Euro targets given to salespeople for an untested, newly launched product that was not suited to the type of clients the organisation typically worked with.

Zone of optimal
performance

Increasing
alertness

Performance

Stress/Anxiety

Boredom

Panic

Physiological Arousal

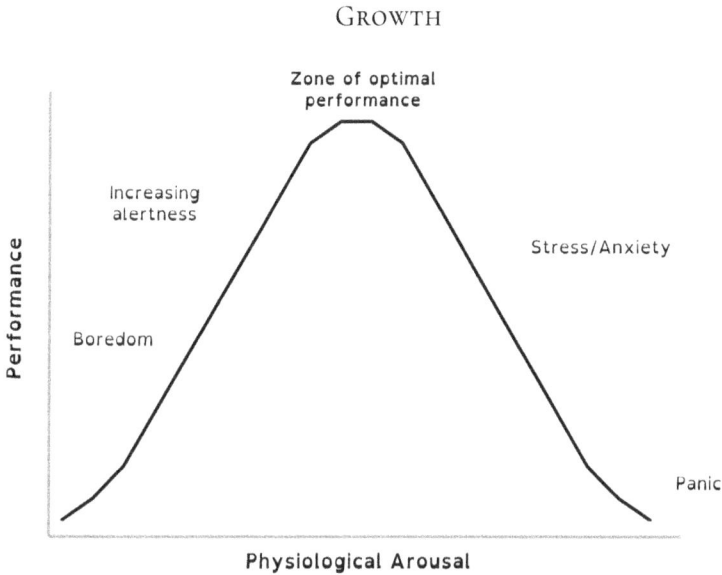

Individual and team goals need to be stretching enough to interest and motivate, but not so stretching that the team members believe they are impossible and give up. The figure below illustrates the 'Yerkes-Dodson Law', which suggests that increased physiological arousal is beneficial to performance, up to the zone of optimal performance. I heard this described as the 'Goldilocks zone' the other day, which I liked. Apparently, it's an astronomy term, but I think it suits people too – like Goldilocks, we want not too little and not too much.

In this zone, we are alert, engaged and still have access to all the different parts of our brains that work together to help us solve problems, make decisions, collaborate with others, etc. Some people refer to this zone as being in 'flow'. We become strongly engaged in the task because it is our sweet spot of physiological arousal and interest.

Once we go past this zone and our nervous systems become overly activated, our performance declines. We start to move into the fight, flight or freeze response where our access to the prefrontal cortex (where our cognitive skills, creativity, speech and language processing takes place) is compromised.

A team of psychologists looked at the interaction between goals and systolic blood pressure (SBP), which is the measure of our bodies being ready to act. They found that if a goal is easy to attain, we get a spike in SBP. If it is moderately hard but feels achievable, we get a larger spike. If the goal seems impossible, our system writes it off and we see a decrease in SBP. When we know a goal is too hard, we deal with it by detaching from it and it no longer motivates us – we have moved into freeze.

What makes this interesting in a team is that everyone will have a different zone of optimal performance. What is exciting and motivating for one person may be boring for another and overly stressful for someone else. This means their reactions to goals and their performance will differ depending on factors such as their personality, skill level, confidence, the task, etc.

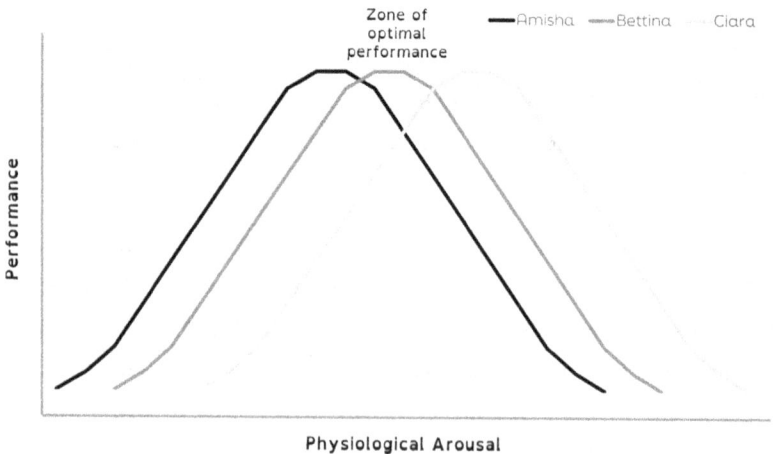

The challenge for the team leader and the team is to understand where each individual's zone of optimal performance lies and to align goals with those individual differences. Goals need to be stretching enough to engage our nervous systems but achievable enough that they don't challenge us to a point where we become overly stressed or switch off completely.

Growth Mindset

'Growth mindset' is an idea pioneered by Stanford professor Carol Dweck. It has become a bit of a buzzword but is often not particularly well understood. A growth mindset (a belief that talents can be developed) contrasts with a fixed mindset (a belief that talents are innate gifts that cannot be developed).

The figure below captures some of the differences between the two mindsets.

Fixed vs Growth Mindset

Fixed Mindset		Growth Mindset
I want to prove I am good	Learning	I want to improve and get better
I don't ask for it and I ignore it if given	Feedback	I ask for it and see it as a source of useful information
I don't want it	Help and Advice	I ask for it
I should know the answer, and don't let it be known when I don't	Knowing the answer	I don't always know the answer, and I don't mind saying so
I find it threatening	Success of others	I find it inspiring
I avoid it	Challenge	I enjoy and seek it
I am afraid of making them	Mistakes	I see them as a source of learning

Ironically, people often misunderstand growth mindset in that they think it is fixed – that you either have it or you don't. But it is actually situational: you can have a fixed mindset about one thing (I can't parallel park so I don't even try) and a growth mindset about another (I often get lost, but I can learn to read maps).

The trick is to identify when we are in growth or fixed mindset mode and what impact that is having. For example, I have been undertaking a three-year course in developmental trauma therapy. As someone with over twenty years consulting and coaching experience I assumed that I would have lots of transferable skills. But I found after a year that I was really struggling. I had reached a certain point in my skill development, and had definitely plateaued.

I was being hampered by my inner voice that criticised my progress, and I could see that I was definitely in 'proving' mode. I was trying to prove to myself and my fellow trainees that I was good at this (after all, I had lots of similar experience, so I believed I should be). The problem was that the style of therapy was actually very different from my coaching and consulting experience; it was far more unstructured and intuitive, and I was having to unlearn a lot of behaviours.

A breakthrough came when I realised I was getting in my own way. My ego was too involved, and I was in proving mode. I saw that I needed to let go and adopt a beginner's mind so I created a mental picture of me sitting at the feet of my teachers as a way of reminding me of the need for humility. I also decided that I needed to practise more, and deliberately sought out ways of practising in a safe, supportive environment.

Being completely honest, I was surprised how effective it was. I found that my internal chatter about how good I was (or should be) massively reduced, and I found it much easier to ask for help and advice. In turn, my skill level increased.

Cultivating a growth mindset can be particularly hard when your self-image is tied to your expertise. It is much harder to admit you have something to learn when you have been doing that thing for many years, especially when it is part of your identity and where you get your confidence from.

Growth mindset is related to the concept of Intellectual Humility whereby we are able to separate our egos from our ideas (see Adaptability chapter), and also to the concept of Psychological Safety whereby the team feel safe to be vulnerable in the group (see Teams chapter).

An inclusive high performing team embraces a growth mindset as much as possible. Team members will tend towards having a growth mindset about a range of things and the team will collectively work to create a team climate that encourages this mindset. This includes using mistakes as learning opportunities, rewarding effort (not just outcomes), building a feedback culture, and challenging team members when they show a fixed mindset. One particularly key element is the ability to make mistakes without being punished. It has come up a few places in this chapter. I want to highlight how important it is that team members feel they can admit to making mistakes so that (a) they can be quickly rectified and (b) the individual and the team can learn from them.

The exercise at the end of the chapter will help your team develop their mindset around mistakes.

EVERYDAY ACTIONS TO BUILD GROWTH IN YOUR TEAM – FOR TEAM MEMBERS

- Share development opportunities across the team. This may mean passing on opportunities that are offered to you.
- Review who your 'point people' in the team are. Try to work with a broader selection of team members, even if that means that you work with people who are less experienced. It may be an opportunity for them to develop new skills.

- Pay attention to your own development, and the development of your colleagues.
- Create a feedback culture by regularly asking for feedback from your team members and other colleagues.
- Don't be afraid to offer feedback to colleagues if you feel it will help with their development. Think carefully about how to give it in a way that is easy for them to hear and action. Remember Situation, Behaviour, Impact (SBI).
- Take a moment to reflect on whether you feel more comfortable giving feedback to some colleagues than others. If you do, why is that? What can you do to create more equity in the feedback you share?
- Praise your fellow team members. Let them know what you appreciate about them. Thank them for their contribution. Just because something is a person's job doesn't mean you can't thank them for doing it.
- Have a growth mindset – focus on *im*proving not proving. Challenge team members who show a fixed mindset.
- Admit when you don't know something. Ask questions and be curious.
- Challenge goals that are too easy or too stretching. Aim for the zone of optimal performance.
- Focus on continuous improvement. Carry out genuine 'without blame' reviews.
- Ensure the team pays attention to how you work together. Don't only focus on tasks.

EVERYDAY ACTIONS TO BUILD GROWTH IN YOUR TEAM – FOR TEAM LEADERS

- Review who your 'point people' in the team are. Give development opportunities and stretch assignments to a broader selection of team members.
- Question your judgement of people on the team. Have you made assumptions about anyone that mean you don't take risks on them?
- Get to know everyone in your team. What are their strengths and development areas? What are their career goals? Are there projects or activities they can get involved in that will help them to develop?
- Role model a focus on personal development. Pay attention to your own development and make sure the team know you are doing it.
- Create a feedback culture by regularly asking for feedback from your team members and other colleagues.
- Choose a simple feedback model (for example Situation, Behaviour, Impact – SBI) and encourage your team to use that model when giving feedback. There is a link in the references to a helpful blogpost on different feedback models.
- Don't be afraid to offer feedback to team members if you feel it will help with their development. Think carefully about how to give it in a way that is easy for them to hear and action. Don't leave it until the annual appraisal cycle – regular feedback is important.
- Praise your team members. Let them know what you appreciate about them. Thank them for their contribution.

- Role model a growth mindset – focus on *im*proving not proving.
- Challenge team members when they demonstrate a fixed mindset. Encourage them to see challenges and mistakes as learning opportunities.
- Don't be afraid to admit when you don't know something. Just because you are the boss doesn't mean you have to know everything. Challenge yourself to role model vulnerability by asking questions and being curious.
- Allow team members to not know the answer. It is ok for them to go away and find out.
- Set team and individual goals that are neither too easy nor too stretching – aim for the zone of optimal performance. Get to know your team members and where their zone of optimal performance lies.
- Focus on continuous improvement. Carry out 'without blame' reviews. Ensure that mistakes are seen as opportunities for learning not punishment.
- Ensure the team pays attention to how you work together. Don't only focus on tasks. Regularly spend time focusing on team development. Use the exercises in this book to develop your team.
- Reward effort and people who take on challenges in order to grow.

TWO QUESTIONS TO MEASURE GROWTH IN YOUR TEAM

You can ask your team members to score the team using two questions. Ask them to give scores from one (Never) to five (Always).

1. Are the team comfortable giving and receiving feedback? Is there a focus on development for individuals and the team?
2. Is it ok to not know the answer and to make mistakes? Does the team have a focus on growth and continuous improvement?

TEAM DEVELOPMENT EXERCISES TO DEVELOP GROWTH IN YOUR TEAM

Here are two exercises that you can use with your team to develop the Growth cluster. The first is for Development and the second is for Improvement. You can facilitate them yourself or ask a member of the team to do it. See Chapter Six for further information about facilitating team exercises.

GROWTH CLUSTER: DEVELOPMENT EXERCISE

'Feedback' Activity

The purpose of this activity is to help the team become more comfortable with giving each other feedback – to share praise and developmental feedback more easily between team members. It is also an opportunity to discuss creating a feedback culture in the team.

This exercise requires longer than many of the others. Many people find it a challenging activity, and you need to give enough time for the one-to-one conversations to happen and for people to decompress and debrief as a group afterwards. I recommend allocating at least ninety minutes.

I also recommend doing it later in your development journey, once the team have started to build trust and are more comfortable with each other, with speaking their minds, and with doing this type of team exercise. If you make this part of an away day, consider doing it in the afternoon and some other, less challenging exercises in the morning to warm up and relax the team and build psychological safety.

The exercise also develops behaviours from other clusters such as Respect (treating each other with respect) and Trust (developing comfort with potential conflict).

You can download this exercise and the team member handout via the Liberare Consulting website – a link can be found at the back of the book.

Team Pre-work - estimated time 30 minutes:

1. Share the 'Feedback' handout with the team and ask them to complete it in advance of the session.
2. Ensure the team know they will be discussing the pre-work in the team session, so it is important they complete it beforehand and bring it to the session with them.

Facilitator Pre-work – estimated time 60 minutes:

1. As the facilitator you will not be joining in the session so you do not need to complete the worksheet, but do spend some time thinking of examples of feedback you have received (both positive and negative) that you found helpful (even though it may have hurt at the time).
2. Re-read the chapter on Growth to remind yourself why you are doing this exercise, and to identify the key messages you want to share with the team.
3. Ensure you have plenty of space in the room you will be using, enough for people to sit in twos and not be

overheard. Set up the room beforehand if you can. You need enough chairs for everyone in the team and they should be set up in pairs – so if you have ten people in the team, you need five sets of two chairs.

4. Figure out how long you will need for the activity. It is set up like speed-dating: everybody has five minutes with everyone else in the team, plus you need to factor in one minute between each 'speed-date' for people to move around. So, if you have ten team members you will need at least 9 x 6 minutes (54 minutes) for the activity, plus intro (5 minutes) and group debrief (at least 15 minutes).

5. There are additional instructions for this exercise as the set-up can be complicated. Download the exercise instructions via the Liberare Consulting website (you can find the link on the last page of this book). It includes full instructions for how to work out who speaks to whom in each round, which is surprisingly complex! I recommend drawing up a visual (like the ones in the downloadable exercise instructions) to help people understand the flow.

6. It can be helpful to have a visible timer, perhaps projected onto a screen. A bell or whistle can let people know when to move to their next feedback partner.

At the Team Session – 5 minutes intro, 60 minutes (estimated) activity, 15 minutes (minimum) debrief: see above to calculate the actual time needed

Introduce the reason for the activity (5 minutes)

You might say something like: We have committed to becoming an inclusive high performing team. This means we need to get comfortable giving and receiving regular feedback between team members. This exercise is an opportunity to develop our skills at both giving and receiving feedback.

Empathise with the team, because they may find this a challenging exercise. Remind them that feedback is a gift – it is information about somebody else's perspective. With information comes choice.

Share a personal story about feedback you have received that has proved helpful in your career. What was helpful about the feedback (both the content of the feedback and the delivery)?

Remind them about and get their agreement to confidentiality. What is discussed in the room stays in the room. They can share their personal story and experience outside the room, but they should not share anything that anyone else has said or done.

Start the activity (60 minutes)

Allocate a letter to each person and get them to sit in their pairs for the first round.

Tell them they have five minutes per round – 2.5 minutes for each person to share their feedback. Tell them you will let them know when the first 2.5 minutes is up, so they know to swap.

Start your timer for five minutes. Let the group know at 2.5 minutes that they need to make sure both people give feedback.

After five minutes ring your bell/shout loudly to let people know to move to their next pairing.

Repeat until everyone has spoken to everyone else in the team.

If you have a large team, you may want to give them a five-minute break part way through so that they can reflect and make notes.

Debrief as a group (15 minutes minimum)

- How did you feel giving feedback?
- How did you feel receiving feedback?

- What did you learn from this session?
- How can we incorporate this learning to build a feedback culture in our team?

Keep the Momentum Going

The aim of the session is to build the team's confidence with feedback and to identify ways to give and receive feedback on a more regular basis individually and collectively.

Therefore, make sure you implement any ideas and plans you agree during the session and regularly review them to ensure they work as intended.

There are several suggestions in this chapter about ways to build a feedback culture that you could consider for your team.

You may find it helpful to repeating the exercise regularly to continue building team confidence and comfort with feedback.

GROWTH CLUSTER: IMPROVEMENT EXERCISE

'My Greatest Mistake' Activity

The purpose of this activity is to help the team become more comfortable with being vulnerable – talking about their mistakes and what they learnt from them. To learn that it is ok to focus on *im*proving rather than proving all the time.

The exercise also develops behaviours from other clusters such as Respect (treating each other with respect) and Trust (being able to ask 'stupid' questions).

You can download this exercise and the team member handout via the Liberare Consulting website – a link can be found at the back of the book.

Team Pre-work – estimated time 30 minutes:

1. Share the 'My Greatest Mistake' handout with the team and ask them to complete it in advance of the session.
2. Ensure the team know they will be discussing the pre-work in the team session, so it is important they complete it beforehand and bring it to the session with them.

Facilitator Pre-work – estimated time 60 minutes:

1. Complete the worksheet yourself too. In fact, I recommend thinking of a couple of mistakes you have made, including funnier ones, and what you learnt from them in advance of the session. It is essential that you role model vulnerability during this session.
2. Re-read the chapter on Growth to remind yourself why you are doing this exercise, and to identify the key messages you want to share with the team.
3. If you wish to, you could purchase a prize to award to the person who made the best or funniest mistake. If you are going to do this, let the team know there will be a prize for the best mistake.
4. If you are not the team leader, talk to the team leader in advance. Tell them that you will ask them to go first in the exercise to role model vulnerability.

At the team session – 5 minutes intro, 30 minutes activity, 15 minutes debrief

Introduce the reason for the activity (5 minutes)

For example, you could say: We want to be an inclusive high performing team and that means we need to continually grow and improve. In order to do that we have to be ok with not always knowing the answer, with making mistakes, and taking learning from our mistakes. This is part of developing our growth mindset. This activity gives us an opportunity to be vulnerable and to share our best mistakes.

If you are awarding a prize, tell the team that there will be a prize for the mistake judged the best one – and take a vote at the end (you can agree your own definition of what 'best' means).

Remind them about and get their agreement to confidentiality. What is discussed in the room stays in the room. They can share their personal story and experience outside the room, but they should not share anything that anyone else has said or done.

Note that this can be a difficult experience for some people so as the facilitator it is a good idea to share one of your mistakes as part of the introduction. You don't have to go into much detail, but a short story showing your vulnerability is a good way to help the team relax. This is particularly important if you are the team leader.

Start the activity – (30 minutes, assuming up to eight team members having three minutes each, plus time for voting)

This is a whole team activity – there are no breakout groups unless you have a large team and there isn't enough time for each person to share; in which case, split the team into two or more breakouts (or have a longer session for the activity).

Ask each team member to share with the team a short summary of what they wrote in their pre-work. Let them know they have three minutes to share their story and you will stop them after three minutes (to make sure everyone has time to share their story and no one person takes up too much time).

When everyone has spoken, ask the group to vote for the best story (keep it simple – just get people to raise their hands) and award the prize.

Debrief as a group (15 minutes)

Get a group discussion going by asking the following questions:

- What did you learn from this session?
- How can we incorporate this learning to build growth mindset in our team?
- Is there anything you'd like to see me do differently (if you are the team leader) to help with this?

Use the GARU model to help you plan:

- Goal – what have you decided needs to be done? What is your goal?
- Action – what action(s) need to take place in order to achieve this?
- Responsibility – who is going to take responsibility for making it happen? Who else will be involved?
- Update – when will they report back on their progress to the wider team?

Keep the Momentum Going

Ensure that any agreed actions are completed and reported back to the team.

Some teams create a regular prize-giving for the best mistakes. This helps create levity and a regular reminder that mistakes are for learning not punishment.

REFERENCES

A Complete List of Feedback Models (Saberr.com) - https://blog. saberr.com/how-to-give-good-feedback

Don't Prove Yourself, Improve Yourself Video (Chip Conley) - https://www.youtube.com/watch?v=p7Jrg4Cwnmw

Feedback: The Powerful Paradox (Zenger & Folkman) - https:// zengerfolkman.com/wp-content/uploads/2019/08/Feedback-the-Powerful-Paradox_WP-2019.pdf

Find The Coaching In Criticism - Harvard Business Review (Sheila Heen and Douglas Stone, 2014) - https://hbr.org/2014/01/find-the-coaching-in-criticism

High Performance Podcast – Katherine Ryan Episode 210 - https://open.spotify.com/episode/3cO636B6Ew9T2yDKz3c2rf?si=a628374a486b4602

How continuous improvement can build a competitive edge - McKinsey - https://www.mckinsey.com/capabilities/people-and-organizational-performance/our-insights/the-organization-blog/how-continuous-improvement-can-build-a-competitive-edge

How to Achieve a Continuous Improvement Culture in Your Team - Nulab - https://nulab.com/learn/project-management/how-to-achieve-a-continuous-improvement-culture-in-your-team/

How to Create a Culture of Feedback - NeuroLeadership Institute Podcast - https://neuroleadership.com/portfolio-items/create-feedback-culture-nov2017/

No Rules Rules: Netflix and the Culture of Reinvention (Hastings & Meyer, 2020) - https://amzn.to/3SMqLtK

The Secret Resume Podcast - Episode 3 - https://www.podbean.com/ew/pb-cwbaq-1386434

Using neuroscience to make feedback work and feel better (Rock, Jones and Weller, 2018) - https://www.strategy-business.com/article/Using-Neuroscience-to-Make-Feedback-Work-and-Feel-Better

When Feedback Meets Diversity - Harvard Business Review (Meyer, 2023) - https://hbr.org/2023/09/when-diversity-meets-feedback

CHAPTER 4

ADAPTABILITY

"In the midst of chaos there is also opportunity."

— *SUN TZU*

WHY IS ADAPTABILITY IMPORTANT?

Organisations, teams, and individuals can get so focused on achieving a particular goal that changing course seems impossible and anyone who suggests a deviation can be seen as not being a good team member. But the VUCA world is constantly changing, and it is absolutely essential that teams can respond to external events.

Organisations like Kodak failed to adapt to change, sometimes even when the need for transformation was staring them in the face.

The Kodak story is an interesting one. They started as an innovative company that took risks on new technology. Their founder, George Eastman, took significant risks in the earlier days of the company, moving from dry plate to film in 1884 and investing in colour film in the 1930s. By the 1950s they were the market leader in the amateur film market. With the invention of the Kodak #1 camera, they were the company that made photography accessible to the masses.

However, from the 1970s onwards, they ignored multiple opportunities to innovate and adapt. For instance, it was a Kodak engineer who invented the first digital camera in 1975. He is quoted as saying the response from Kodak management was 'that's cute – but don't tell anyone about it'.

In 1981 when Sony introduced the first electronic camera, Kodak's market intelligence team conducted research identifying that digital photography had the potential to replace Kodak's film-based business, but that it would take some time and Kodak had around ten years to prepare.

Except they didn't. Despite information to the contrary, they continued to envision a future where people would use film and want to print out their photographs. They didn't like what they perceived as an enormous threat to their business, so they stuck their heads in the sand, ignored the problem and surrounded themselves with people who thought the same way they did.

When their CEO retired in 1989, rather than replacing him with someone who might bring a different perspective, someone who understood digital technology and could lead them into a new and different future, they chose someone who said he would 'make sure Kodak stayed closer to its core businesses in film and photographic chemicals'.

This pattern went on for many years. It's not that Kodak didn't invest in digital technology: they did, but they were too slow. A company video found on YouTube (link in the references) trumpets their innovative ideas for digital photography, which might have been exciting if it hadn't been made in 2007 when digital cameras had been widely available for at least ten years.

If we compare the Kodak company with their main competitor, Fujifilm, it is interesting to see their completely different approach from Kodak. They also saw the demise of film and chose to diversify their business into adjacent areas such as pharmaceuticals and cosmetics (which from the outside may seem very different, but, like manufacturing film, involve chemicals). They also went into more obviously aligned areas such as healthcare imaging and developing a film used in the production of LCD screens. In 2004 they developed a six-year plan with a goal of 'saving Fujifilm from disaster and ensuring its viability as a leading company with sales of two or three trillion yen a year.'

The Kodak company saw change as a threat and were unable to envision a future that was different from the one they knew. They filed for bankruptcy protection in 2012 and re-emerged as a smaller company in 2013. Their 2021-22 turnover was $1.205 billion (around £975 million), compared with nearly $16 billion (£12.7 billion) in their peak year of 1996, when they were considered the fifth most valuable brand in the world.

The Fujifilm company saw change as an opportunity and re-invented themselves. In 2021-2022 they had turnover of 2.5 billion yen (about $20 billion or £13.5 billion) with its camera and imaging business representing only around 13% of revenue.

The Adaptability cluster in The Inclusive Team™ model captures the need for teams to respond to external forces, to be agile and innovate... to be more Fujifilm!

There are two sub-clusters in the Adaptability cluster, the first of which is Flexibility – the ability of the team and individual members to adapt and change according to need. The second is Innovation – an essential aspect of a team's ability to respond to change by coming up with new and creative ideas.

SUB-CLUSTER: FLEXIBILITY

The Flexibility sub-cluster deals with the ability of individuals and the team to adapt to change. This includes a view of outside factors that may impact the team and its goals, which requires taking a systems thinking approach and acknowledging that the team is not an island – it operates in a complex system, both within the organisation and the outside world.

Flexibility links closely with the Alignment cluster in that external forces may necessitate a rapid change in direction. The team need to both identify the new direction and ensure they are all aligned.

Systems Thinking

Many teams I have worked with are too internally focused, failing to recognise that they are part of a much larger, complex system. This may be because of a desire for simplification and to focus only on what they believe they have control of, but often the result is that their progress is slowed because they failed to consider the external forces that will potentially influence what they are trying to achieve.

We may not be able to control the outside world, but we are impacted by it, and we ignore it at our peril. A favourite quote of mine is from Jon Kabat-Zinn: 'You can't stop the waves, but you can learn to surf'. This helps us stop trying to resist the inevitable forces of change and to learn to thrive in the new place we are being taken to.

The system can be viewed like a many layered onion with the team at the centre (see example below). They need to be aware of activity in all the layers to be able to adjust and flex their actions in response to information and changes in the other layers. If we don't engage with the other layers, we may operate in an echo chamber and are much more likely to be subject to groupthink.

The layers of your team's onion may differ from the ones in the image below. Your customers may be internal and form one of the inner layers, for example. The principle still stands. The team is part of a system that will influence the success of the team, and you ignore it at your peril.

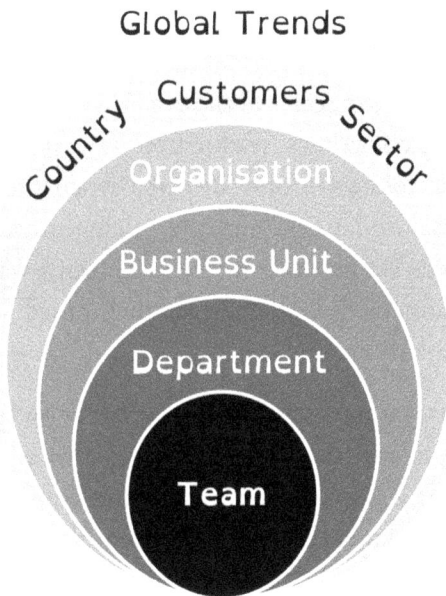

For example: a Learning and Development team launched an all singing all dancing online introduction to management course, only to find take up was extremely low. This was due in part to the launch of mandatory training by the Health and Safety team at the same time, and many leaders saw this as a priority. By not keeping up to date with the plans of other departments, and by failing to understand their customers' (the organisation's employees) priorities, the L&D team failed to achieve the participant numbers they were anticipating. Fortunately, the team were able to re-launch much more successfully at a later date.

A more costly example is the product launch of an online tool designed to complement a popular leadership diagnostic, helping leaders apply the learning from the feedback diagnostic. In theory it was a good idea, as applying the learning and keeping momentum are typical challenges leaders face when receiving feedback from a diagnostic. Part of its appeal was that it was supposed to reduce the time an organisation's learning and development team needed to devote to follow up support and coaching.

The design was kept top secret in the organisation, only involving a few people in the company's headquarters. Local teams who were going to sell the tool were only involved when the product was complete, just before launch, and the pricing/marketing strategy had been decided. Feedback from the local teams was not considered prior to launch, despite the fact they raised some genuine concerns, particularly around price.

The product was not successful. Clients saw it as overpriced, particularly since people were used to getting similar tools for free, or for a nominal sum. It was overly complex for users, and it required far more human involvement and support from the clients' Learning and Development teams than anticipated.

One client summed it up perfectly: *'It looks like you got a bunch of really clever people in a room to design the tool and didn't talk to anyone who was going to use it.'* The product never met its ambitious sales targets and was quietly withdrawn.

The product development team had failed to look outside their team for feedback and perspectives from colleagues in other parts of the business, or from the customer. When feedback was received it was ignored, even though some of it (e.g. pricing) would have been easy to change.

Cognitive Dissonance

Once teams have received feedback or identified challenges to their progress, they need to quickly integrate the information into their current world view and be flexible enough to respond rapidly. This may mean anything from a slight change of plan to a wholesale re-think of an idea or strategy.

I often see teams and individuals make the mistake of ignoring or disparaging information that does not fit into their world view. There are two key, related psychological elements that we all experience at play here: cognitive dissonance and confirmation bias. When we understand these habits, we can identify when we (or other team members) are falling under their spell, and then decide if they are helpful or not.

We all view the world from a particular perspective. We have beliefs, attitudes and values and our minds do not cope well with information contrary to our world view. We call this cognitive dissonance. It is the sense of discomfort we feel when we try to hold two seemingly contradictory things in our mind. We perform mental gymnastics to try to resolve the dissonance and reduce our discomfort.

People tend to cope with cognitive dissonance in several common ways:

- Adopting beliefs/ideas that help us justify or explain the conflict.

- Hiding our beliefs/behaviours from others.
- Seeking out information that confirms our existing beliefs, and ignoring information that doesn't. This is known as confirmation bias. We tend to pay attention to information that is in alignment with our world view and ignore information that is not.

In a team who are very focused on a particular goal but receive information that their plans may be flawed in some way, these behaviours could look like:

- Disparaging the source of the information ('they don't know what they are talking about'; 'they aren't our target market, so we don't care what they think'; 'they're just lazy').
- Ignoring the information completely (avoiding the source of information so they don't have to engage with it).
- Minimising drawbacks ('they're exaggerating the problem'; 'there are so many variables, we can't take everyone's feedback into account').
- Trying to work quickly and away from others so they can't see what is going on and 'interfere'.
- Engaging only with supporters (seeking out people who confirm their world view – creating an echo chamber).

Joan Schneider and Julie Hall say in an HBR article about product launches (see references), 'Managers must learn to engage the brand team and marketing, sales, advertising, public relations, and web professionals early on, thus gaining valuable feedback that can help steer a launch or, if necessary, abort it. Hearing opposing opinions can be painful—but not as painful as launching a product that's not right for the market or has no market at all.' The story I gave earlier of the failed online tool is an example of feedback not being sought and the product and price being wrong for the market.

I know the development and launch of products does not involve all teams, but the principle is the same regardless of the type of work the team does. We do not work in a vacuum, and it is essential we engage with the system to know what is going on that will potentially impact our goals.

One of the advantages of having a diverse team is that you are likely to have a better collective understanding of the system. Each team member will bring a range of experiences and perspectives of what is going in on the different layers in the system. This is particularly true if your team has experience of working across the system, for instance in different parts of your business or sector.

At the end of this chapter you will find an activity to help your team analyse their system and the way it impacts the team.

System Wide Relationships

Building relationships with people outside the team is an essential part of giving the team an insight into what is happening in other parts of the system. Too often teams rely on their leader to be the bridge between themselves and the rest of the system, but in a high performing team each team member takes responsibility for actively building relationships.

There are two main benefits to this. Firstly, the relationships are a source of information to help you identify activities, initiatives and trends that may impact the team's ability to achieve its objectives. These external forces could be headwinds that delay your progress, or tailwinds. There may be complementary initiatives you can collaborate on that could provide a boost to what you are trying to achieve.

Relationships are by far the best way to achieve this, because you are often able to find out about things well in advance of official communications. The official structures of an organisation are not how most work gets done. Power and influence do not necessarily go hand in hand with position and status, and a team that knows how to tap into informal networks gets things done faster and more effectively than one that rigidly follows official structures and processes.

These informal lines of communication allow your team to be aware of what is going on across the system and be agile in the way that you plan and carry out your work.

The second benefit of building system wide relationships is they can often make delivering your work smoother and quicker. There are multiple aspects to this:

- Knowing who the right people are to get things done (this is different from the point people in your team – this is knowing who in your network is responsible for different activities).
- You can influence stakeholders to identify and potentially overcome resistance.
- We are more likely to do favours for people we know and like and tend to do things more quickly, therefore if we build relationships, we may be able to call in favours and get things done more easily or quickly.
- If you are looking to achieve system wide change, you can use those relationships to build a network of people who work on your behalf across the system. You can build up a critical mass of supporters. See the Organisational Implementation chapter for more on this.

I certainly found my job in a large consultancy easier after I had worked in several different teams and departments. The relationships I had developed across the business meant I could call someone up and ask them for a favour (we are much more likely to go out of our way for someone we know and like). I also gained a better understanding of the day-to-day concerns of different parts of the organisation which meant I could influence stakeholders across the business by appealing to what I knew was important to them.

My personal experience is reinforced by the regular feedback I receive when I review cross-organisational development programmes. Without fail, one of the key things the participants say that they appreciate and have benefited from is the opportunity to get to know colleagues from across the organisation. They say it gives them a network of colleagues they can reach out to for advice and support, and that it makes their day-to day-work easier.

Flexibility of Team Structure

Much of our focus so far has been on responding to external forces outside our control that have an impact on the team's goals and strategy. However, flexibility within the team structure is also important when change happens. This links closely with the Alignment cluster – where team members feel a shared responsibility for success of the team.

The ever-changing organisational environment that teams work within means that team structure rarely stays the same. It is often fluid with team members leaving and joining at different times. This can cause disruption and slow progress. Thus, if the team is to work at maximum efficiency, they need to help new members get up to speed quickly and feel part of the team.

This may seem obvious and logical, but in fast paced, performance driven organisations, I often see new team members left to sink or swim on their own. Sometimes they are lucky to get opportunities that allow them to integrate with the team, but other times they are left out with nobody taking time to properly onboard or integrate them.

Focusing on welcoming and aligning the new team member helps them feel like they belong and are part of the in-group, which helps create the environment for more collaborative, innovative team-work. This is explored in more depth in the Alignment chapter.

Particular attention needs to be paid to integrating a new team member who is different from the rest of the group. They are less likely to feel like a member of the in-group if they look or sound different, or have a different background from the rest of the team.

My friend John once told me about the time he joined a new organisation. John has a great corporate job now but grew up in a lower income working-class environment. On his first day at his new job, he was talking to one of his new colleagues (Sarah) and they were interrupted by another colleague (Jeremy) who wanted to say hello. Sarah and Jeremy hadn't seen each other for some time, and they began sharing stories of their vacations in their holiday homes in exotic locations. Not only did they exclude John from the conversation by talking just to each other and not inviting him to join in, but they unintentionally made him feel like a complete outsider by talking about shared experiences that were only available to people with significant personal wealth. As they were some of the first people he had met at the organisation, it made him wonder what kind of business he had joined, and if everybody was from a very different background from him.

This is a good example of a micro-behaviour (you can read more about those in the Respect chapter) where Sarah and Jeremy hadn't meant to make John feel different and excluded, but their behaviour and choice of conversation was unintentionally exclusive and made John feel even more like an outsider than he already did.

It is often considered the role of the team leader to ensure a new team member is well integrated. However, in inclusive high performing teams, all team members consider it their duty to incorporate new team members properly, because they understand that this helps the whole team perform better.

Closely linked to this is the ability of a team to respond rapidly to changes of direction and workload demand. This could mean a permanent restructure or reallocation of resources to respond to a change in direction. Or if the change is temporary – for example, a sudden spike in workload in one part of the team – that the other team members offer support and resources.

I have seen this work quite well in the UK Civil Service. When significant external events require a rapid deployment of resource (e.g., Covid response, Brexit planning, London 2012 Olympics), departments from across government will free up resources to work on a temporary basis on the urgent project. They are released on secondment, and I believe are guaranteed a job when they return to their home department.

The people who go on secondment often get the additional benefit of a fantastic opportunity to learn new skills, build new networks and learn about a different part of the system. They then bring that learning back to their home department.

I know the solution often isn't perfect, and the Civil Service are constantly looking at ways to improve it, but it works a lot better than many other organisations I have seen where one part of the business is on its knees, and the other parts feel no responsibility for supporting and ensuring its success.

This again links with the Alignment cluster – it will only happen when all team members feel responsible for the success of the entire team, not just the goals that they are personally responsible for.

SUB-CLUSTER: INNOVATION

This may sound similar to the Improvement sub-cluster in the Growth chapter. However, whereas Improvement is about small incremental improvements, setting goals and being stretched, this sub-cluster is about finding new and creative ideas that ensure that teams thrive in the VUCA world. They are nevertheless related. As William Pollard said, "Learning and innovation go hand in hand. The arrogance of success is to think that what you did yesterday will be sufficient for tomorrow."

Innovation is one of the most talked and written about aspects of organisational life. If you search the Forbes website for 'innovation' you will get over 120,000 results, and many leadership gurus have highlighted the importance of organisations being innovative. Peter Drucker wrote, "We can already see the future taking shape. But I believe the future will turn in unexpected ways. The greatest changes are still ahead of us... To survive and succeed, organizations will have to become change agents. The most effective way to manage change successfully is to create it."

The challenge many organisations face is that they don't focus enough on creating the environment that encourages innovation. Silo working, a focus on short term results and efficiency, internal competition, and individual reward structures all act as counter forces to innovative behaviours. This is often replicated within teams, where there is often a strong focus on individuals achieving the task in hand in the most efficient and timely manner, with little time, energy or space given to new or radical ideas.

Innovation requires a shared mindset that the need to innovate, flex and grow is part of the team's remit. That innovation is not solely the responsibility of the R&D department, but that knowledge and fantastic ideas are to be found right across the organisation, in every individual and every team.

The Innovation sub-cluster combines three factors. The first is that curiosity and bringing new ideas is encouraged. The second is the way the team behaves when new ideas are expressed – they build on and try to understand the ideas and perspectives of their teammates to access their collective intelligence. The third and final factor that differentiates high performing teams is that they have an execution mindset so that new ideas are actually implemented not just discussed.

Curiosity

Innovative teams foster curiosity. Albert Einstein once said, "I have no special talents. I am only passionately curious." In a high performing team, team members encourage each other to bring their ideas to the group, no matter how wacky they might seem.

There is a Zen Buddhist concept called Shoshin, also known as 'beginner's mind' which refers to the idea of letting go of your preconceptions and having an attitude of openness when studying a topic. We do this naturally as children, but as adults, our knowledge and expertise tend to block us from seeing things in a new way. In the words of Zen master Shunryo Suzuki, "In the beginner's mind there are many possibilities, but in the expert's, there are few."

How often have you caught yourself thinking in a meeting or on a workshop, "Oh, I already know this," and switching off? This is really the time we need to listen even harder. There may be a new spin on what we already know, or an additional five percent that is missing from our understanding, which we will miss if we have zoned out.

I started a podcast at the beginning of 2023 (*The Secret Resume* Podcast), and many of my initial guests were people I already knew. Or at least I thought I did. What has been fascinating to me is how much I have learnt about these people by sitting down and interviewing them for an hour – focusing on asking them questions and letting them tell me about their lives. I had made so many incorrect assumptions about them, and there were whole, important parts of their lives that I had no idea about.

The software I use to transcribe the interviews tells me what percentage of the time each of us was speaking, and my aim is for the guest to speak eighty percent or more. This tells me I'm not interjecting my ideas and thoughts too frequently, and the interview isn't becoming about me. I also ask the guests to identify the key points we are going to talk about. The podcast is about their story, the way they want to tell it, rather than the story as defined by the questions I choose to ask from my narrow perspective.

Steve Jobs famously gave a speech in 2005 at the Stanford University graduation ceremony (or Commencement Address as it's often known). He talks about following his 'curiosity and intuition' when he dropped out of college and started going to classes that interested him rather than his required curriculum. One of these classes was calligraphy, which may have seemed like a somewhat random choice, but which influenced him strongly ten years later when he designed the first Macintosh computer. He said, "It was the first computer with beautiful typography. If I had never dropped in on that single course in college, the Mac would have never had multiple typefaces or proportionally spaced fonts. And since Windows just copied the Mac, it's likely that no personal computer would have them."

Innovative teams need to give time and encouragement to team members to be curious, not just about the immediate task at hand, but about what's going on in other parts of the organisation, and what is coming on the horizon. This also means being interested in and having a perspective on the work of other team members. There is no 'stay in your lane', because all the lanes are the responsibility of all the team.

This can feel difficult in a world where we are all running at one hundred miles per hour and overwhelmed by the huge amount of information available to us. I frequently see leaders advised to focus and refine and reduce their engagement with 'spurious' information. Whilst I understand the rationale in that it helps people concentrate on what needs to be done, with it comes a danger that we miss a lot of potential connections. Information that may seem unrelated at the time may be of immense help further down the road. The ability to connect seemingly unrelated pieces of information is a real skill and is seen by many as one of the indicators of leadership potential.

I realised looking back at my career that the things that have had the biggest **impact** on where I am today came at times when I followed my curiosity and wandered off the expected path, such as when I gave up my first managerial job to go and live in a ski resort in Canada, or later when I moved out of the consulting part of my organisation and into a section of the business considered less important and glamorous.

In Canada, I worked for a man who helped me identify my love of developing others, which has been my focus for over twenty years. When I moved out of the consulting team, I got much more involved in marketing, picking up knowledge and skills I would never have learned as a consultant and are fantastically helpful to me now I own my own business.

Accessing Collective Intelligence

The collective intelligence of the team is influenced by the diversity of ideas and perspectives in the team, combined with the ability of the team to work together to create something bigger and better than any one of those individual ideas.

When someone shares an idea with the group, it is essential the idea isn't immediately shut down. This requires team members to be open to discussing the idea and trying to understand and build on it.

The presence of lots of different perspectives can trigger cognitive dissonance in team members (discussed earlier in this chapter). For cognitive elaboration (see below) to take place, individuals need to learn to sit with their cognitive dissonance and not perform the mental gymnastics that we often do to ensure our world view is not altered.

There are several related concepts that can help us.

Intellectual Humility

This is the acceptance that your beliefs and opinions could be wrong. Researchers Liz Manusco and Stephen Rouse describe it as having four elements:

- Respect for others' views.
- Not being overconfident in your ideas.
- Ability to separate your ego from your intellect.
- Being willing to revise your views.

So often in teams we see each individual being very attached to their ideas and unable to back down and accept that someone else's perspective may be correct. This tends to lead to an inability to truly hear what the other person is saying, as the individual is usually trying to defend their idea and formulate a response whilst the other person is talking. It is easy to spot this in others but can be much harder to admit that we also do this ourselves (I know I do!).

This is an essential component of team innovation. We cannot truly create new and radical ideas if we each stick rigidly to our own perspectives – if our ego and self-image are too closely tied to our beliefs and to being 'right'.

I have always found it frustrating when colleagues or clients criticise their competitors, implying that what the competition do is sub-standard and that their way is the 'right' way. I have always been intensely curious about what competitors do well. I want to know what we can learn from them and apply in our own company. If we are too rigidly attached to our way being the best way, we miss opportunities to find alternative and maybe better ways of doing things.

Cognitive Elaboration

Cognitive elaboration is the process of sharing, challenging, and expanding our thinking. It contributes strongly to teams (particularly diverse teams) benefitting from their diversity and collective intelligence. It includes behaviours such as openly exchanging information and ideas, seeking clarification on the perspectives offered by others, and discussing and integrating this information.

It is the difference between saying 'yes, but' and saying 'yes, and'. The former discounts what has been previously said, and the latter builds on what has been said. Some teams I have worked with have deliberately built a team habit of saying 'yes, and' instead of 'yes, but' when responding to something another team member has said. They do this in order to ensure that team members build on each other's ideas rather than dismissing them and just putting forward their own point of view.

We need to be careful that it is genuine – you can't just substitute the word 'and' when you really mean 'but' – it has to be a genuine build on what the other person has said. Similarly, saying 'building on what Anne just said' and making a completely unrelated point is also not cognitive elaboration!

Perspective taking

One key team behaviour that impacts cognitive elaboration is perspective taking. This is where team members attempt to understand the thoughts, motives, and feelings of another person. We naturally have an egocentric view of the world, and it is not easy to move away from that and step into seeing the world from another's perspective. This is particularly true if that person is very different from us and their view seems a long way from our own, which is likely to be the case in diverse teams.

It takes both a desire to take the perspective of another, and practice to be able to do this effectively. An exercise at the end of this chapter will help your team develop this skill.

Relationships

The team's ability to innovate is also related to the system-wide relationship building that we discussed in the Flexibility sub-cluster in this chapter. Greg Satell is a well-known writer on innovation and change and recognises the value of establishing broad networks outside the team to boost innovation.

He believes that in our modern, complex world the best innovators are not lone independent geniuses who lock themselves in a dark room to come up with radical ideas. He suggests that '...the best innovators tend to be knowledge brokers, who embed themselves into networks so that they can access that one elusive piece of insight that can crack a tough problem'.

He also says that those networks are not just in our organisations. 'To compete effectively today, we need to be able to access ecosystems of talent, information and technology that lie far beyond the bounds of our organizations. In effect, the best of everything lies somewhere else.'

The system-wide relationships we build let us gain insights that allow us to be agile and flexible and to implement solutions easily. A relationship may also be the source of a vital piece of information that allows us to develop a radical and innovative solution. Whilst it is helpful for the team to have clear boundaries and clarity about team composition and role, it is also important that their boundaries are permeable when it comes to information flowing in and out. It is an interesting balance between having clarity and confidence in the team and at the same time accepting that there are others outside the team who have useful information and ideas.

Implementation

The final key factor of innovation in high performing teams is implementation. I'm sure we have all worked in teams where lots of great ideas are generated, but they rarely go anywhere, and very little is ever implemented.

I have seen many reasons for the failure to implement ideas, including the fact that ideas are generated in isolation without reference to the wider system in which the team operates, so that when the team tries to implement, they are met with strong resistance.

That resistance could be due to a range of factors including fear, organisational politics, poor change management practices, a company culture that prefers the status quo, or a failure to build enough support with key stakeholders. This reinforces to the importance of the relationship building mentioned above.

Another common reason implementation fails to happen is that the team prefers to discuss and come up with ideas but doesn't have strong implementation skills to turn them into reality.

When we think about team diversity, we can get caught in the idea of diversity of demographics such as gender, ethnicity, etc. However, it also means paying attention to diversity of skills. A team full of people who love to debate and discuss will come up with great ideas but struggle with implementation. A team full of people who prefer to take action are unlikely to come up with radically new ideas. Bringing together these preferences can be hard work and create tension because it can feel like they are pulling in opposite directions. Nevertheless, high performing teams need to be able to ideate *and* implement.

Too often when we build a team we look for 'cultural fit'. What we mean by that is 'will they be easy to work with?' If we really want a high performing team that is innovative and adaptive to our ever-changing world, we must accept that the conflict and friction that comes from a less homogenous team is essential. We instead need to look for 'complementary fit': how will the team members add value to this team? – What do they each uniquely bring that will help the team perform at its best?

In addition to team composition, some simple habits can help move a team towards a more action-oriented state. You may notice in many of the exercises at the end of each chapter that I suggest using the acronym GARU to help with action planning. It also helps create clarity of direction and ownership, the importance of which have been discussed elsewhere in this book. GARU stands for:

Goals – what are we aiming for? What are we trying to achieve?

Action – what actions need to be taken to achieve the goal?

Responsible – who is going to lead on this? Who is going to support?

Update – when will they update the team on progress?

This doesn't have to be a long and painful process; I encourage you to use it quickly and lightly. It is simply a way of creating a clear action for every decision taken in a meeting. If you don't like this, use another one, or make up one of your own. The key is that you create a shorthand or language the team can use to build a habit that will help them focus on implementation.

A NOTE ON INCLUSION

The main focus of this chapter has been building flexibility and innovation to create high performing teams. There is no doubt that having a diverse team will contribute to the team's ability to do both of those.

However, I also want to highlight that elements such as perspective taking, curiosity, intellectual humility and relationship building also strongly influence how inclusive a team feels. They are not only essential components of flexibility and innovation; they are core skills that will help team members develop their understanding of people who are different from them and create an inclusive team where everybody feels they belong.

Everyday Actions to Build Adaptability in Your Team – for Team Members

- Keep connected to trends and initiatives that occur outside your team and share your observations regularly with the wider team.
- Build relationships outside your team and across your system so you are kept up to date on things that will impact your team and can tap in to the collective wisdom outside your team.
- Get to know the unofficial power structures in your organisation. Who do you really need to know to get things done?
- Don't gatekeep resources. If other team members have a greater need than you do for resources, share them across the team.
- Be open to responding quickly to changes in direction.
- Work to create a culture of curiosity and innovation in the team.
- Cultivate your intellectual humility. Try to detach your ideas from your ego and remain open to hearing others' perspectives.
- Practise perspective taking. Take time to understand something through the eyes of another team member or stakeholder.
- Take an active role in integrating new team members into the team. Get to know them on a personal level and help them understand the team's goals, behavioural norms, etc.
- Build on your teammates' ideas rather than shutting them down. Listen carefully to what they say and practise cognitive elaboration – remember 'yes, and'.

- Watch some improvisational comedy to see cognitive elaboration at work.
- Be bold. Bring new ideas to the group, even if they seem a little left-field.
- Encourage your teammates and support them when they bring new and radical ideas to the team. Listen and take them seriously.
- Develop your change management and implementation skills (see Organisational Implementation chapter)
- Identify actions, owners and reporting when ideas are discussed (remember GARU).

EVERYDAY ACTIONS TO BUILD ADAPTABILITY IN YOUR TEAM – FOR TEAM LEADERS

- Encourage the team to keep connected to trends and initiatives that occur outside your team and create opportunities for them to share their observations regularly with the wider team. Give time for them to do this.
- Regularly spend time with the team analysing the system you work in. Identify trends and activities that may impact your team's goals.
- Build a map of key stakeholders (remember that it's not just related to positional power) and agree with the team who will spend time building relationships with each stakeholder.
- Encourage the team to build relationships outside your team (in addition to key stakeholders) across your system so you are kept up to date on things that will impact your team.

- Help the team to understand the unofficial power structures in your organisation. Who do they need to know to get things done?
- Work to create a culture of curiosity and innovation in the team. Recognise and reward team members who demonstrate these qualities.
- Ensure that team members don't gatekeep resources. Share resources and move them around the team as required.
- Be prepared to respond quickly to information that suggests you may need to change direction.
- Cultivate your personal intellectual humility. Try to detach your ideas from your ego and remain open to hearing others' perspectives. Reward and recognise team members who also do this.
- Practise perspective taking. Try to understand something through the eyes of another team member. Encourage team members to do the same.
- Ensure that new team members are integrated into the team. Get to know them on a personal level and help them understand the team's goals, behavioural norms, etc. Make sure the rest of the team is involved in this.
- Encourage the team to build on each other's ideas rather than shutting them down. Role model cognitive elaboration.
- Role model boldness. Bring new ideas to the group, even if they seem a little left-field, and recognise team members who do the same.
- Ensure there is a forum for team members to share their ideas.
- Build your change management and implementation skills. Ensure the team has members who have strong implementation skills.

- Place a focus on implementation. Identify actions, owners and reporting when ideas are discussed (use GARU or come up with your own acronym).
- Build a team that has complementary skills and experiences, even if it means that it will feel less comfortable at times.

TWO QUESTIONS TO MEASURE ADAPTABILITY IN YOUR TEAM

You can ask your team members to score the team using two questions. Ask them to give scores from one (Never) to five (Always).

1. Does the team respond quickly and flexibly to external events that impact its goals?
2. Does the team focus on creating and implementing new and innovative ideas?

TEAM DEVELOPMENT EXERCISES TO DEVELOP ADAPTABILITY IN YOUR TEAM

Here are two exercises you can use with your team to develop the Adaptability cluster. The first is for Flexibility and the second is for Innovation. You can facilitate them yourself or ask a member of the team to do it. See Chapter Six for further information about facilitating team exercises.

ADAPTABILITY CLUSTER: FLEXIBILITY EXERCISE

'Megatrends Onion' Activity

The purpose of this activity is to build their skills in looking outside the team at external trends that currently have an impact on the team and identifying those that may have an impact in the future.

The exercise also develops behaviours from other clusters such as Alignment (linking team activity to organisational strategy) and Growth (focus on continuous improvement).

You can download this exercise and the team member handout via the Liberare Consulting website – a link can be found at the back of the book.

Team Pre-work – estimated time 30 minutes:

1. Share the 'Megatrends Onion' handout with the team and ask them to complete it in advance of the session.
2. Ensure the team know they will be discussing the pre-work in the team session, so it is important they complete it beforehand and bring it to the session with them.

Facilitator Pre-work – estimated time 60 minutes:

1. Complete the handout yourself so you can share your thoughts in the workshop, but also so you can answer the team's questions when they are filling it out.
2. Read and understand the instructions in full. You may decide that the titles in the layers of the onion are incorrect for your team. You could change the titles if you want to ensure they all do the exercise exactly the same. Alternatively, you could let them interpret it themselves, which could lead to some interesting discussions.
3. Read the Introduction (for information on VUCA and Megatrends) and the Adaptability chapter to ensure you are familiar with the concepts being discussed and why

you are focusing on the Flexibility sub-cluster with the team.

At the Team Session – 5 minutes intro, 30 minutes activity, 15 minutes debrief

Introduce the reason for the activity (5 minutes)

You might say something like: We have committed to working towards becoming an Inclusive high performing team. This means we need to look outside our team to understand the system we work in and identify things that may have an impact on what we do as a team.

Remind them about and get their agreement to confidentiality. What is discussed in the room stays in the room. They can share their personal story and experience outside the room, but they should not share anything that anyone else has said or done.

Start the activity (30 minutes)

- Split the team into breakout groups of around four people.
- Ask them to analyse the onion layer by layer, sharing their thoughts from the pre-work.
- Request that they nominate someone to feed back key themes to the larger group.

As the facilitator you do not join a group. You can check they understand the instructions, but do not get drawn into the discussion. This is particularly important if you are also the team leader, as it would be very easy for you to become the focus of the conversation, rather than the ideas and perspectives of the group.

Debrief as a group (15 minutes)

Go round the small groups asking them to share their key themes:

- What activities or trends did they identify in the different layers?
- What impact could that have on the team?

When you have heard from all the sub-groups, ask the whole group:

- What key themes do we see?
- What does the team need to do to respond?
- How do we take this forward?
- How do we ensure we continue to look outside our team to identify trends and activities that may impact us?

Use the GARU model to help you plan:

- Goal – what have you decided needs to be done? What is your goal?
- Action – what action(s) need to take place in order to achieve this?
- Responsibility – who is going to take responsibility for making it happen? Who else will be involved?
- Update – when will they report back on their progress to the wider team?

Keep the Momentum Going

This is not a once and done activity. Scanning the external environment and building relationships within that environment is an important aspect of being a high performing team.

In addition to actions you identify as part of the group debrief, repeating this exercise on a regular basis will ensure you maintain a focus on the system the team operates within.

ADAPTABILITY CLUSTER: INNOVATION EXERCISE

'Perspective Taking' Activity

The purpose of this activity is to help the team build their collective intelligence by improving their ability to look at problems from different perspectives.

The exercise also develops behaviours from other clusters such as Trust (differences of opinion are encouraged), Alignment (creating a shared sense of responsibility), Growth (paying attention to the way the team works together) and Respect (treating each other with respect).

You can download this exercise and the team member handout via the Liberare Consulting website – a link can be found at the back of the book.

Team Pre-work

There is no pre-work for team members for this exercise.

Facilitator Pre-work – estimated time 60 minutes:

1. Re-read the chapter on Adaptability to remind yourself why you are doing this exercise, and to identify the key messages you want to share with the team.
2. As the facilitator make sure you read and understand the instructions in full.
3. Download the handout and print enough copies so that each team member has a copy.

At the Team Session – 5 minutes intro, 35-40 minutes activity, 15 minutes debrief

Introduce the reason for the activity (5 minutes)

You might say something like: We have committed to working towards becoming an Inclusive high performing team. This includes using our collective intelligence to innovate.

Perspective taking is a key skill when coming up with new ideas: it is the ability to understand the world from another person's perspective. This exercise will help us practise that skill by asking us to understand the perspectives of our team-mates.

Remind them about and get their agreement to confidentiality. What is discussed in the room stays in the room. They can share their personal story and experience outside the room, but they should not share anything that anyone else has said or done.

Start the activity (35-40 minutes)

Give them the handout and walk them through the exercise.

Split the team into breakout groups of three (no more than four if your numbers don't divide by three). If you have groups of four the exercise will take slightly longer than if you have groups of three.

As the facilitator you do not go into any of the small groups. You can wander around and check if they have any questions, but do not get drawn into a long conversation with any group. Your key task here is to help them keep on track by giving them time checks: there are multiple stages to the exercise, and it would be easy to spend too much time on one task:

- After three minutes, remind them to move on to the individual work (step two).
- After thirteen minutes, remind them to move on to the first small group discussion (step three).
- After 28 or 33 minutes (depending on whether the groups are threes or fours), remind them to move on to identifying themes (step four).
- After 33 or 38 minutes (again depending on group sizes) close the small group exercise.

Debrief as a group (15 minutes)

Go round the small groups asking them to share their key themes:

- How easy/difficult was the exercise and what made it easy/difficult?
- What did they learn from this session about themselves and about the team?

Ask the whole group: How can we incorporate this learning to make our team more inclusive (as individuals and collectively)?

Keep the Momentum Going

Look for and recognise/reward perspective taking when you observe it in meetings.

Perspective taking is not just important within the team – it is important to understand the perspectives of key individuals or stakeholders outside the team. This can be a helpful exercise to repeat with a focus on trying to tune into the perspectives of key stakeholders.

References

4 Ways to Build an Innovative Team - Harvard Business Review (Greg Satell, 2018) - https://hbr.org/2018/02/4-ways-to-build-an-innovative-team

Cultivating Curiosity Is What Drives Innovation (Sarah Austin, 2020) - https://www.entrepreneur.com/leadership/cultivating-curiosity-is-what-drives-innovation/351487

How Kodak Failed - Forbes (Chunka Mui, 2012) - https://www.forbes.com/sites/chunkamui/2012/01/18/how-kodak-failed/

Peter Senge Explains Systems Thinking - YouTube Video - https://www.youtube.com/watch?v=eXdzKBWDraM&t=3s

Steve Jobs Stanford Commencement Address (2005) - https://news.stanford.edu/2005/06/12/youve-got-find-love-jobs-says/

The key role of dynamic talent allocation in shaping the future of work - McKinsey, 2021 - https://www.mckinsey.com/capabilities/people-and-organizational-performance/our-insights/the-key-role-of-dynamic-talent-allocation-in-shaping-the-future-of-work#/

The Secret Resume Podcast - https://thesecretresume.podbean.com/

This Zen Concept Will Help You Stop Being a Slave to Old Beliefs (James Clear) - https://jamesclear.com/shoshin

What is Intellectual Humility? How it Works and How to Develop it (Shane Snow) - https://shanesnow.com/research/what-is-intellectual-humility-how-it-works-and-how-to-develop-it

Why Most Product Launches Fail - Harvard Business Review (Joan Schneider and Julie Hall, 2011) - https://hbr.org/2011/04/why-most-product-launches-fail

CHAPTER 5

RESPECT

"Treat everyone like a brother, even if you've never met them before."

— *HECTOR GARCIA & FRANCESC MIRALLES,*
IKIGAI

WHY IS RESPECT IMPORTANT?

In the introduction, I highlighted some of the benefits of creating a diverse and inclusive team, including better performance, avoiding groupthink, and greater levels of innovation. This is about benefiting from the collective intelligence of the team; some call it accessing the 'diversity dividend'. Whilst there are elements of inclusive behaviours woven throughout The Inclusive Team™ model, this cluster draws out some of the most important actions required to create a diverse and inclusive team. The Respect cluster reinforces the idea that it is not enough to bring diverse individuals to the team. A diverse team that isn't inclusive will not thrive. It will clash, and performance will be affected. The differences of perspective and approach will become an irritant, causing confusion and conflict. This is one reason why it is important to focus on inclusive team behaviours, not just inclusive leader behaviours. All of the team need a shared belief in the value of diversity, and to appreciate the differences their colleagues bring, even if that difference is sometimes challenging.

There are two sub-clusters in the Respect Cluster. The first is Diversity. Do the team members share the perspective that team diversity is important? Is there a focus on developing relationships and understanding each other, and do they respect the diverse needs of the team? The second sub-cluster is Belonging. This is team members treating each other in a respectful manner, making an effort to ensure people feel able to be themselves and calling out non-inclusive behaviours.

SUB-CLUSTER: DIVERSITY

At a very basic level the diversity sub-cluster is about building a team with a broad range of diverse characteristics, rather than recruiting in our own image or people we think will 'fit' and are easy to get on with. It means being brave and choosing team members who complement the existing team – who bring something different, who may disagree. But what do we really mean by diverse characteristics?

Diverse Characteristics

When people think and talk about diversity in organisations, there is a tendency to focus on a few characteristics such as gender, race and ethnicity, LGBTQ+ and disability. For example, in the UK, there are nine characteristics which are legally protected from discrimination under the Equality Act 2010 (often referred to as the 'protected characteristics'). These are Age, Disability, Gender reassignment, Marriage or civil partnership, Pregnancy and maternity, Race, Religion or belief, Sex and Sexual orientation.

Other countries have similar lists of protected groups, which may vary by state or territory. It is important you understand the equality laws for your country/region/state.

Organisations tend to focus on the characteristics that are protected by law rather than thinking more broadly about what diversity really is. This can lead to a compliance mindset where organisations do the bare minimum to ensure they don't break the law.

I find it helpful to take a much more expansive view of diversity and recognise the huge range of things that make us special and unique. In 1990, diversity consultant Marilyn Loden and academic Dr Judy B Rosener developed a 'Diversity Wheel' framework for thinking about the many dimensions of diversity. This framework can help people understand that DEI is for all, not just people with protected characteristics. It helps people get in touch with their own experiences of feeling 'other', builds empathy, and increases engagement with the challenges of creating a more diverse and inclusive culture. It can also help people (who may look and behave quite differently on the surface) connect through shared diversity characteristics they were previously unaware of.

This has been replicated and adapted many times over the years, and below is the version we use at Liberare Consulting. You can find a larger colour image in the book downloads available via our website – the link is on the last page of this book.

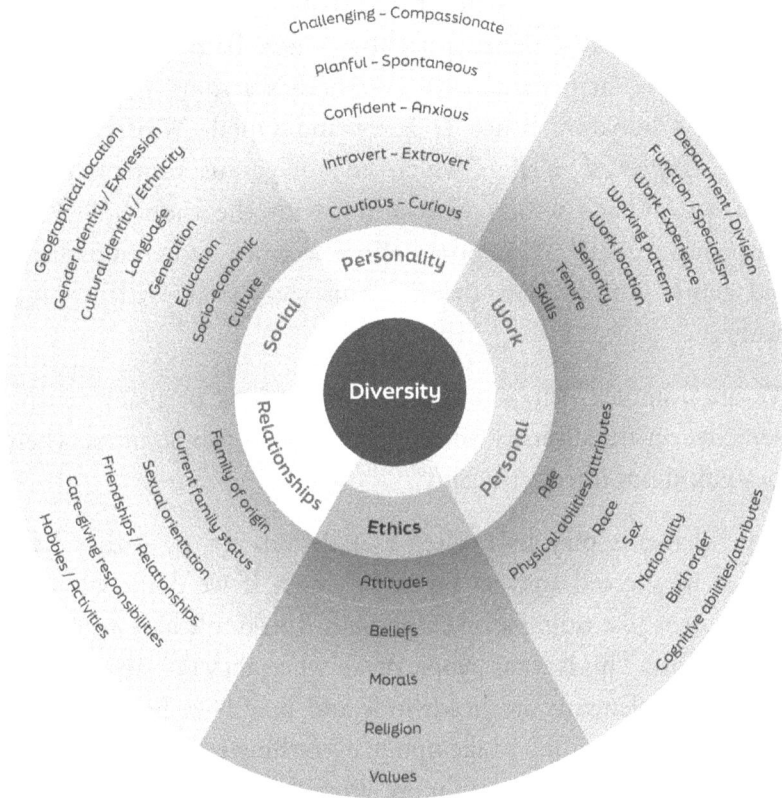

This model shows how our different elements of diversity can be grouped into six clusters: Personality, Work, Personal, Ethics, Relationships and Social.

Some aspects are visible to others, and some are invisible and would need to be shared for others to know this about us. You can think of it as people being like icebergs or trees – only a percentage is visible to others, but the aspects that are not visible are equally as important. It is easy to judge people and make decisions based on the visible aspects, but it is really important that we remember everyone has things about them and life events that we don't know about or understand.

I'm a great fan of the quote from theologian, Ian McLaren: 'Be kind, for everyone you meet is fighting a hard battle.' It recognises that invisible factors influence everybody's actions. I also really enjoyed a book by Bruce D Perry and Oprah Winfrey called *What Happened to You?* which encourages us to replace the thought, 'What's wrong with you?' with the thought, 'What happened to you?' This puts us into a much more empathetic and gently curious state that takes us away from criticism and blame.

We are complex beings and are combinations of many of the elements on the diversity wheel. This is what people mean when they talk about intersectionality.

Some elements may have acted as tailwinds for us – they have helped us succeed and get on in life, even if we don't know it. Think of it like riding a bike downhill: you don't have to put in much effort. This is what people mean when they talk about privilege. Some elements are headwinds and may have held us back. That can be like riding a bike uphill: everything is just that little bit harder, and we have to put in more effort to be successful.

All the aspects of our diversity have influenced the way we see the world, our experiences, and the perspectives we bring. This is why a diverse team can be more innovative and tackle complex problems –it has access to a broad range of experiences and viewpoints, so can come up with new and unique ways and ideas to solve problems.

A word of caution about introducing the diversity wheel: I have seen people use it as an excuse for not focusing on specific demographic groups or to convince themselves that their team is more diverse than it actually is. The challenge is to simultaneously hold the idea that we all have experiences of feeling different and 'other' (we all have headwinds and tailwinds that have influenced our life) *and* recognise that some groups have historically experienced many more headwinds than others.

I haven't worked with any organisation that doesn't have noticeable under-representation of women, certain ethnicities, people with disabilities, members of the LGBTQ+ community, and people from lower socio-economic groups. The under-representation may not be throughout the organisation, but it is almost always seen at leadership levels. This is where the Equity part of DEI really comes into play. We may need to take actions that recognise years of systemic headwinds so that we level the playing field in the team and organisation.

My recommendation is to use the diversity wheel as a tool for engagement and awareness, but don't let it become a blocker to placing focus on specific groups.

Valuing Diversity

When we talk about creating a diverse team, we aim to bring a range of different perspectives and experiences into the group. It is about respecting diversity, not performing a tick box exercise, understanding the value that diversity can bring and actively seeking to bring difference into the team.

It is not about pretending that diversity doesn't exist ('I don't see colour' or 'I don't think about you as a woman') which is how some people may have been taught to think or talk about difference. The problem with pretending to ignore specific characteristics is manyfold.

For one, what we say is probably not really true (we do see colour!) and we are just trying to convince ourselves, to say what we think is the right thing, or to move away from an uncomfortable topic. Secondly, if we really want to get the best from our diversity, we need to recognise and celebrate it – we can't do that by pretending it doesn't exist. Thirdly, it's often quite insulting to the individual on the receiving end of these comments. It feels like the other person is diminishing your experience, your value, and in particular the headwinds you may face because of your gender, race, disability, etc. If you say you don't see something, then you also can't empathise with their challenges or value what that element of difference brings.

I worked with the senior leaders in an organisation (let's call them Organisation B), the majority of whom had the perspective that it's none of their business what religion someone is (for instance) or whether they are a member of the LGBTQ+ community. Therefore, they wouldn't ask. They believed they were coming from a positive position of tolerance ('It's none of my business, and I don't care what religion you are, or who you are attracted to.') rather than a position of respecting and valuing an individual's difference.

When asked to review the diversity of their social circle at work using the diversity wheel, they simply didn't know some quite fundamental things about their colleagues. Many found it difficult to see that their apparent lack of interest could be perceived as pushing things under the carpet, that their colleagues may have avoided talking about things that were important to them because the culture of 'don't ask, don't tell' created an undercurrent where some things felt inappropriate or shameful to discuss. This may have led to masking or covering behaviours which have a negative impact on an individual's engagement and wellbeing. This is particularly true of invisible aspects of diversity. We discuss this further in the Belonging sub-cluster later in this chapter.

I always tell my clients that tolerance is not enough. In an inclusive high performing team, individuals are curious to know more about their colleagues. They want to know them as people, to understand their experience and point of view, and how that differs from their own.

Inclusive Team Norms

The final aspect of the Diversity sub-cluster is the respect for the diverse needs of the team when it comes to team events/celebrations/meetings etc. This means understanding that different team members have different preferences and needs that should be respected. Examples include:

Timing of meetings. Parents who have to do school drop off might find an 8.30am meeting difficult, for instance. Global teams have an additional challenge because of time zones, and I note that individuals in the Asia/Pacific region often come off worst from a time zone perspective when working in global teams. Some teams I have worked with alter the times of their regular meetings so that no one time zone is impacted more than others. A good example of inclusion comes from a team I am working with as I write this book. They have asked that I run some focus groups at times that work for their staff who regularly do the night shift. They are some of the most disengaged colleagues, and their perspective is often missed out because they can't attend meetings in regular working hours.

Team socialising. Some people do not drink for religious or other reasons and feel uncomfortable if team socialising always takes place in a bar where alcohol is served. Other people have specific requirements when it comes to food. Creating social events that do not all revolve around alcohol and ensuring that a range of food is available are simple ways of creating a more inclusive way for colleagues to socialise and bond with each other.

Training. The rapid increase in online training since the Covid-19 pandemic has had a positive impact on inclusion for many groups.

Removing the need to travel and be at face-to-face training is positive for many groups including people with disabilities and people with caring responsibilities. I remember once speaking to a woman who was considered high potential, but she would not apply for her organisation's high potential scheme because she lived in Northern Ireland and the majority of the training was face to face in England, which would mean several weeks away from her family.

Accessibility. When people imagine someone with a disability, they typically think of a person with a visible physical disability, such as someone in a wheelchair. However, wheelchair users are only eight percent of disabled people in the UK, with eighty percent of disabled people having hidden impairments. To be inclusive, consider if colleagues have accessibility requirements. For instance: Are venues accessible for physically disabled colleagues? Are your documents compatible with screen readers? Are the acoustics challenging for people who have hearing difficulties? Do you give dyslexic colleagues sufficient time to read and absorb information before responding?

Celebrations. Team members will choose to celebrate different events, sometimes related to their religion but also linked to other aspects of their diversity (for instance Pride month for the LGBTQ+) community. For instance, in the UK, we can't assume all team members want to celebrate Christian holidays. Some may have religious practices (such as fasting during Ramadan) and may benefit from different working patterns. Inclusive high performing teams are respectful and aware of a range of religious and cultural celebrations; they not only make adjustments but acknowledge and celebrate with their colleagues.

The list above gives a very small number of examples. There are many more ways of ensuring your team culture and norms take the team's diversity into account so that everybody feels welcome. It is highly individualised, and no list can ever cover every situation. Therefore, the first step is to ensure the team feel comfortable disclosing and discussing their diversity and sharing what would make them feel more comfortable and included in the team.

Organisation B that I mentioned above would never be able to do this, because their position of 'don't ask, don't tell' meant nobody felt safe to disclose any aspect of difference; therefore, changes couldn't be made, even if the organisation wanted to. The Diversity Wheel exercise at the end of this chapter is a great way of getting this conversation started.

Sub-cluster: Belonging

The degree of respect in a team relates to a sense of belonging: 'Do I feel valued and that I belong here?' It is about team members feeling they can be themselves and can drop the mask that so many under-represented groups feel they have to put on at work. It is not necessarily about 'bringing your whole self to work' (some people may not want to), but about feeling that you can bring whatever you want, and that you don't have to hide aspects of yourself for fear of being judged or ostracised. Belonging is a fundamental human need. We are tribal mammals that rely on each other to survive, and social pain – the experience of being excluded or rejected – lights up the same regions of the brain as physical pain.

Organisations also benefit from creating environments where people feel they belong. Research by Better Up found that high levels of belonging were linked to a 56 percent increase in job performance, a fifty percent drop in turnover risk, and a 75 percent reduction in sick days. Their research also suggested that people who feel excluded work less hard for the team, even if it means they are personally impacted.

Masking

Masking is a term often used to describe how neurodivergent people (for instance, those with ADHD or autism) actively change their behaviour to cover up parts of themselves that might make them seem too different from others. Examples would be managing their energy so as to not appear too fidgety or that they talk too much. Whilst the concept of masking is most often associated with neurodiversity, other minority groups report that they also mask in order to fit in. Ethnic minorities may culturally mask, by not wearing traditional dress or hairstyles, for example, or toning down their direct style so as not to be labelled as the 'angry black woman' stereotype. Members of the LGBTQ+ community may not be 'out' at work, and feel they have to conceal their same sex relationships for fear of being judged (this is sometimes referred to as 'covering').

I am a single parent and talk openly about my experience. However, I was surprised when I was approached by multiple women after a personal branding workshop I facilitated. They shared with me that they were shocked at how open I was. They kept their single parent status a secret at work for fear of being judged and people making assumptions about their dedication and aspirations.

Masking is exhausting. It takes a lot of mental energy to act in ways that are at odds with our natural tendencies or to cover up parts of our lives by outright lying or avoiding talking about things or people that are important to us. This energy could be more usefully focused on team goals and tasks, and this would have a positive impact on team performance. One of my podcast guests (see link in references) gives an example of how different and more authentic she feels at work now that she feels able to be open about her same-sex relationship.

The more significant aspect of masking is the impact on our mental health. When we internalise the lack of respect for a part of ourselves, we can start to feel shame about it. This can lead to anxiety and depression. Research at the Universities of Albany and Exeter found that concealing stigmatised characteristics (e.g. LGBTQ+, history of mental or physical illness, history of poverty) led to a reduction in self-esteem, job satisfaction and commitment at work.

In homogenous teams, the perceived need for masking is likely to be low as the team will have similar backgrounds, experiences and perspectives on the 'right' way to behave or be. In diverse teams where Respect is low, it is likely that a lot of masking is going on and having a negative impact on team members and the team's performance.

This isn't to suggest that in high performing teams everyone behaves exactly how they want all of the time. That could be chaos, and part of being in a successful team is learning how to work with and get along with others. That may mean all of us dialling up and down different aspects of our personalities and self-expression to meet the team's goals. Authenticity is not about being yourself all the time without regard for the feelings or perspectives of others.

Authenticity does mean getting to know each other on a human level – learning about our differences and how those differences show up at work. It is about understanding another's experience and creating an environment where they feel safe enough to drop the mask, even if it's not all the time.

Micro-behaviours

A respectful team will understand how micro-behaviours can have an impact on how included team members feel. Micro-behaviours are small, often subtle and unconscious gestures, comments and behaviours that may have a different impact from the one we intended. I think of micro-behaviours as our bodies 'leaking' what we really think and feel. They often reveal our unconscious biases to others, even if we don't notice them ourselves. They can have a positive (micro-affirmations) or negative (micro-aggressions) impact.

Micro-affirmation examples include:

- Active listening (nodding, making affirmative noises) when someone speaks.
- Calling out when someone is interrupted.
- Making eye contact.
- Asking for someone's opinion.

Micro-aggressions examples include:

- Taking a phone call in the middle of a conversation or meeting.
- Frequently forgetting someone's name.
- Assuming a role/hierarchy based on how someone looks (e.g. assuming the only man in the meeting is the boss).
- Talking over or interrupting someone.

Our intent is often not to make someone feel excluded by a micro-aggression, but the impact can be exactly that.

Micro-behaviours in our language can inadvertently create a non-inclusive environment. Language is incredibly powerful and can be both unifying and divisive; it can be a hot topic of conversation as everybody has a different opinion about what is appropriate. Inclusive language in a team setting has many elements, including:

- Respecting an individual's pronouns (most commonly we use he/she/they, but there are many others that individuals may use. See references for a link to the Stonewall guide).
- Restricting use of jargon and acronyms. This is particularly excluding for new team members or people outside the team who might struggle to keep up with the conversation.
- Using genderless language, for example 'team' or 'folks' or 'everyone' instead of 'guys' (which implies that men are the preferred gender).

It is a complex and often passionately debated topic, as I was reminded only a few days ago while having dinner with friends, as there are no hard and fast rules or answers. Different people have different perspectives on 'correct' language, and it is inevitable that at some point you will say something that someone doesn't like. However, this doesn't mean you shouldn't try, and I have provided a link to a handy inclusive language guide in the references section if you want to dig a little deeper.

My final piece of advice around inclusive language is to not get too caught up in extended discussions. It is easy to spend many hours debating something that is often down to preference; you are not going to be able to entirely satisfy everyone. Long debates can get in the way of taking meaningful action and driving change in the team or organisation.

Challenging non-inclusive behaviour

One of the challenges of being inclusive is that our unconscious biases are just that – unconscious. We often aren't even aware that we have them, and we don't notice when we are acting on them. They leak out in our micro-behaviours, for instance. This is why a respectful team has a culture where it is safe to speak up if you notice non-inclusive behaviours in others or are on the receiving end of bias.

When we challenge non-inclusive behaviour, we are helping the perpetrator understand their own biases, which gives them a chance to change. If we are the perpetrator, the person who challenges us is doing us a favour and helping us become more aware of our own biases and the impact our behaviour has on others. If we are an observer of non-inclusive behaviour (neither the perpetrator nor the recipient of the behaviour), by challenging it we are being an ally to the person who was negatively impacted. An ally is someone who has moved beyond an awareness of DEI and actively supports and advocates for their under-represented colleagues.

Challenging someone on non-inclusive behaviour is one of the most powerful things we can do to create an inclusive high performing team, but it's also one of the most difficult. We've all been there: someone says something inappropriate, and we really want to say something, but we don't and often kick ourselves afterwards. I still replay occasions in my head when I wanted to speak up and I didn't – such as the time a colleague described a client as a 'ball-breaker' because she was insistent on including women in shortlists for senior roles. In truth, I did speak up, but not clearly or decisively enough to be sure they understood what was wrong with what they said.

There is strong social pressure to not rock the boat or call someone out, particularly if the statement was said as a joke or 'banter'. Our desire to be part of the in-group and not be seen as the 'fun police' can drive us to stay silent. We don't challenge because we don't want other team members to judge us, or perhaps we think someone else will intervene (the bystander effect). Or perhaps we second guess ourselves and are not confident that we should get involved, or maybe we don't like conflict and shy away from it.

Often, we don't call someone out because we are afraid to do it in the moment. It seems too conflictual or will embarrass the individuals involved. The model below is a version of the Five Ds, which I believe was developed by the 'Right To Be' organisation and is often used in allyship or bystander intervention training. This gives a range of ways to tackle inappropriate behaviours – you can use one or a combination to deal with non-inclusive behaviour in a way that works best for you and the situation. There is an activity using this model in the team development exercises at the end of this chapter.

Assume Positive Intent

I want to add a final thought on challenging non-inclusive behaviour, which is the suggestion to assume positive intent until proven otherwise.

Discussing DEI can be difficult and challenging. What is offensive and non-inclusive to one person can be perfectly acceptable to another member of the same under-represented group. It is complex and confusing, and people can be afraid to talk about DEI because they are scared of saying the wrong thing or offending someone.

When dealing with non-inclusive behaviour, I would encourage you to approach it from the perspective that the perpetrator is speaking/acting from a place of ignorance not malice. This can place us in a better mindset to have a reasonable conversation with them and be willing to listen as well as share our perspective. If we assume ill-intent or maliciousness, we are likely to approach the same conversation in a different frame of mind. Our ability to listen and have an effective dialogue will be compromised.

I know this is easy for me to write, but less easy to do. If someone has been given feedback and continues to be non-inclusive, then a different conversation needs to be had (hence the importance of documenting so that patterns can be identified).

Having difficult DEI discussions is an important topic. I talk about it in more detail in the Implementation chapters (Chapters Six and Seven).

Presence

The final aspect of respect is the gift of presence, both physical and mental. One of the biggest blockers to team performance is the fact that people don't show up, either physically because they are not prioritising the team, or mentally because they are multi-tasking and trying to do several things at once.

We have all been in meetings where people are answering emails on their phone, or on their laptop – they look like they might be taking notes, but they're really surfing the internet. I was told a story recently by a client who was interviewing a candidate with a colleague. Whilst he was speaking his co-interviewer, who looked like he was taking notes about the interview on his laptop, actually pulled out his credit card to buy something online. In the middle of the interview. My client was mortified, and I can just imagine how the candidate felt!

If a person routinely doesn't show up to team meetings, they are telling you they don't think the collective goals of the team are as important as their other priorities.

If someone turns up and is physically but not mentally present, they are telling you the same thing. It is not possible to multi-task. As much as we would like to believe we can, we simply cannot focus on two things at the same time. When we 'multi-task' we are actually switching rapidly between tasks, which decreases the attention and focus each task gets, giving worse performance and outcomes. Cognitive Psychologist Paul Atchley tells us that research shows multitaskers miss information, and efficiency can drop by as much as forty percent. In addition, multi-tasking has a negative impact on long-term memory, and creativity is reduced.

Technology is a wonderful thing. It gives us flexibility, the ability to work from a beach in Bali, and it has taken away many boring and tedious tasks. I am old enough to remember a time when people didn't have laptops or mobile phones, used overhead projectors instead of PowerPoint, and didn't routinely use email – people could even smoke in offices (but that's a whole other story!). I can absolutely see how technology has benefitted us all; however, it is also a massive source of distraction. It has led us to believe that we can multi-task, that we can go to meetings and still attend to all the other things going on outside of the meetings. Except... we can't.

This is particularly true in virtual meetings. It is very easy to be distracted by email, phones, the dog, or that urgent thing that just has to be done today. If we have our camera off, nobody can even tell if we are listening or not. Except often they can, because usually when we are multi-tasking we are not contributing. If you're going to multi-task throughout the meeting, you might as well not be there because you're not engaging in the conversation and giving your colleagues the gift of your attention and focus.

Lack of physical or mental presence impacts a team in a range of ways:

- Decisions not being made because key people weren't there.
- Longer meetings because discussions have to be repeated because some people were not paying attention at the right time.

- Team members who have committed to being both physically and mentally present feeling frustrated and disrespected.
- Delays further down the line because things were agreed but some people weren't paying attention and didn't put forward their point of view when the decision was made.
- Poor decisions or ideas because key/alternative perspectives were missed.

I could go on!

In simple terms, to benefit from the team's collective intelligence, team members need to be physically and mentally present and contributing.

EVERYDAY ACTIONS TO BUILD RESPECT IN YOUR TEAM – FOR TEAM MEMBERS

- Create a team diversity calendar with your colleagues (you can search for one online) and celebrate a range of things that are important to different team members.
- Be present (physically and mentally) with your colleagues, both in one-to-one dealings and team meetings. Put away your phone/laptop and minimise distractions. Make sure others know you are not to be disturbed and that team meetings take priority in your diary.
- Turn on your camera in virtual meetings.
- Call out non-inclusive behaviours that you experience or observe. If you find that difficult to do in the moment, use the Five Ds model to plan how to do it. Remember, it doesn't have to be in public – a private conversation can often be equally effective.

- Be open to having your non-inclusive behaviours called out. Try not to be defensive and listen carefully to the feedback.
- Be mindful of the language you use. Reduce the use of acronyms and use the correct pronouns for your team members.
- Be curious about your colleagues. Get to know them as people and don't shy away from having discussions about your differences as well as your similarities.
- When recruiting look for complementarity to the team, not similarity. Don't focus on whether someone will 'fit', focus on what difference they will bring to the team.
- Attend Inclusive Recruitment training to learn how identify and manage your biases during the recruitment process for new team members.
- Devote time to learning about diversity, equity and inclusion: read books, listen to podcasts, and talk to people who are different from you.
- Carry out an audit of your work and social circle. Do you live in an echo chamber? How diverse are the people you know and the media you consume? Try to identify where you can broaden the voices you listen to.
- Be respectful towards your colleagues, even if they have a different opinion from you.
- Try to understand someone's intent. Don't jump on them if they say something inappropriate if you think their intent is not to harm or upset – a private word is often more effective than a public roasting.
- Be kind – everybody is fighting a battle that you know nothing about.

Everyday Actions to Build Respect in Your Team – for Team Leaders

- Review the behaviours listed in the 'Team Member' section above: role model them yourself and reward team members who demonstrate these behaviours.
- When recruiting, don't just roll out the previous job description. Check that it reflects what you need in your team now. Look for complementarity – someone who will bring something different to the team, not someone who will just 'fit in'. Ensure that everyone who is involved in the recruitment process (HR/Talent Acquisition/Team Members) understands the need for team diversity and are trained in Inclusive Recruitment.
- Ensure the team have time to get to know each other as individuals rather than focusing on the task the whole time. The exercises throughout this book will help with this.
- Regularly talk about the importance of creating a diverse and inclusive team – why it is personally important to you and why it is important to the team performance.
- Create opportunities for the team to talk about diversity, equity and inclusion in a safe space. Encourage open dialogue, and make sure that people who make mistakes are given feedback and the opportunity to change, not attacked.

Two Questions to Measure Respect in Your Team

You can ask your team members to score the team using two questions. Ask them to give scores from one (Never) to five (Always).

1. Is there a focus on building a diverse team and do the team members value that diversity?
2. Are the team respectful towards each other and do they work to create a team environment where everyone feels valued?

TEAM DEVELOPMENT EXERCISES TO DEVELOP RESPECT IN YOUR TEAM

Here are two exercises you can use with your team to develop the Respect cluster. The first is for Diversity and the second is for Belonging. You can facilitate them yourself or ask a member of the team to do it. See Chapter Six for further information about facilitating team exercises.

RESPECT CLUSTER: DIVERSITY EXERCISE

'The Diversity Wheel' Activity

The purpose of this activity is to broaden the team's definitions of diversity and help the team get to know each other better so that they can understand each other's experiences and perspectives. It also helps them connect to their own experiences of diversity and feeling 'other' which helps build empathy and connection.

The exercise also develops behaviours from other clusters such as Trust (sharing views), and Accountability (getting to know each other's strengths).

You can download this exercise and the team member handout via the Liberare Consulting website – a link can be found at the back of the book.

Team Pre-work – estimated time 30 minutes:

1. Ask the team members to watch one of these videos on YouTube: the Franklin Covey 'All of Us' video or the Heineken 'Worlds Apart' video. You can choose which you think works best. Links are in the exercise instructions that you download (see above).
2. Share the 'Diversity Wheel' handout with the team and ask them to complete it in advance of the session.
3. Ensure the team know they will be discussing the pre-work in the team session, so it is important they complete it beforehand and bring it to the session with them.

Facilitator Pre-work – estimated time 60 minutes:

1. Watch the video and complete the handout yourself so you can share your thoughts in the workshop, but also so you can answer the team's questions when they are filling it out.
2. Re-read the chapter on Respect to remind yourself why you are doing this exercise, and to identify the key messages you want to share with the team.

At the Team Session – 10 minutes intro, 25 minutes activity (if in groups of four), 15 minutes debrief

Introduce the reason for the activity (5 minutes)

You could say something like: Part of becoming a more inclusive team is getting to know each other better so that we can understand each other's experiences and perspectives. As part of developing the team's collective intelligence we need to understand the different experiences and perspectives in the team. We also want to ensure the team is as inclusive as possible, and to do that you need to know what that would mean for each team member.

This is an opportunity for us to get to know each other better, to learn about different aspects of diversity, and to practise listening. (You can share any of the information or research from the Respect chapter that stood out for you to help explain why you think this is important.)

Remind them about and get their agreement to confidentiality. What is discussed in the room stays in the room. They can share their personal story and experience outside the room, but they should not share anything that anyone else has said or done.

As a warmup (to get them talking) ask them what they thought of the pre-work video.

- What messages or lessons did they take from it?
- How does that apply to the team?
- How does it apply to the broader organisation?

There are no right or wrong answers. You just want to get a conversation going about different aspects of diversity.

Ask them how they found completing the Diversity Wheel. Typically people find it interesting, and like the fact that there is a broader way of looking at and talking about diversity. They may also be a little nervous about sharing, particularly if your team hasn't shared much personal information before or if they are new to the team. If this happens, reassure them that they only share what they are comfortable sharing. They don't have to share the whole wheel – just three to five elements that are important to them. Remind them again about confidentiality.

Remind them this is an exercise in getting to know each other better. It is about sharing aspects of ourselves that others may or may not know about us.

Start the activity (25 minutes)

Depending on the size of your team and the time you have available, you could make this a whole team activity or break out into smaller groups. Make sure every person has at least five minutes to share their diversity wheel, plus five minutes at the end to share any additional thoughts/identify themes.

These instructions have been written as though you have split into sub-groups, but you can adjust them to make it work as a whole team exercise.

Ask team members to manage the time so each person has five minutes to be the 'presenter', plus five minutes at the end.

Each person takes it in turn to be the 'presenter' and share three to five aspects of their diversity wheel with their group members. For each item of the diversity wheel they share, they can talk about:

1. Why it is important to them (why they chose to share it).
2. How it plays out for them at work.
3. What would make the team more inclusive for them.

The group members can ask the 'presenter' questions, but they should try to give the person who is 'presenting' space and time to talk and share what they have chosen and why. Remind them that people may be sharing things for the first time, and things that are very personal to them, so listening and respect are important.

Once everyone has had a turn at being presenter, ask the sub-groups to spend five minutes discussing what they learnt, noticing any themes, etc. before returning to the main group. Ask them to nominate someone to present their themes.

As the facilitator, you do not go into any of the small groups. You can wander around and check if they have any questions, but do not get drawn into a long conversation with any group.

Debrief as a group (15 minutes)

Ask someone from each group to share any themes they noticed.

Get a whole group discussion going to identify group learning. You could use the following questions:

- How did you find being the presenter?
- What did you learn from doing the exercise?
- How can we incorporate this learning to make our team more inclusive (as individuals and collectively)?
- Is there anything you'd like to see me do differently (if you are the team leader) to help with this?

You can use the GARU model to help you plan:

- Goal – what have you decided needs to be done? What is your goal?
- Action – what action(s) need to take place in order to achieve this?
- Responsibility – who is going to take responsibility for making it happen? Who else will be involved?
- Update – when will they report back on their progress to the wider team?

Keep the Momentum Going

Some teams create posters to put on the wall that shares information about each individual. Everyone creates their own poster so they can share what is important to them. New team members create their own poster when they join.

Create opportunities for the team to continue to get to know each other informally. For example, I have seen teams create fun processes such as randomly pairing up team members with the expectation they will take a coffee break together (in person or virtually) in the next month. This is repeated each month with different pairings. You could use the handout from this exercise as a conversation guide.

RESPECT CLUSTER: BELONGING EXERCISE

'Tackling Difficult Conversations' Activity

The purpose of this activity is to help the team get more comfortable with tackling non-inclusive behaviours.

The exercise also develops behaviours in other clusters such as Trust (dealing with conflict), and Alignment (holding each other accountable).

You can download this exercise and the team member handout via the Liberare Consulting website – a link can be found at the back of the book.

Team Pre-work – estimated time 10 minutes:

1. Ask the team members to watch the 'It's Not Just Banter' video. The link is in the references section and in the exercise instructions that you can download.

2. Make sure the team know they will be discussing the pre-work in the team session, so it is important they watch the video beforehand.

Facilitator Pre-work – estimated time 60 minutes:

1. Re-read the chapter on Respect to remind yourself why you are doing this exercise, and to identify the key messages you want to share with the team.
2. Download the 'Difficult Conversations' handout' from the Liberare Consulting Website, (link in the back of the book) and print out enough copies so that each team member gets one.

At the Team Session – 10 minutes intro, 20 minutes activity, 15 minutes debrief

Introduce the reason for the activity (5 minutes)

You might say something like: Part of becoming a more inclusive team is being able to challenge non-inclusive behaviours, both within the team and in the wider department/organisation. We know it's sometimes difficult to do that.

(You can share any of the information or research from the Respect chapter that stood out for you to help explain why you think this is important.)

Remind them about and get their agreement to confidentiality. What is discussed in the room stays in the room. They can share their personal story and experience outside the room, but they should not share anything that anyone else has said or done.

As a warmup (to get them talking) ask them what they thought of the 'It's Not Just Banter' video. You can use the following questions:

- What messages or lessons did they take from it?
- How does that apply to the team?
- Have they ever experienced or observed inappropriate comments disguised as jokes or banter?

There are no right or wrong answers. You just want to get a conversation going about how some behaviours might be perceived as acceptable banter by some, but unacceptable by the person on the receiving end.

Start the activity (20 minutes)

Split the team into at least two sub-groups – around three to five people per group – and give them the handout. Ask them to read the case study and discuss the questions. Ask them to nominate a spokesperson to share back some key messages when you return to the main group.

As the facilitator you do not join a group. You can check that they understand the instructions, but do not get drawn into the discussion. This is particularly important if you are also the team leader, as it would be very easy for you to become the focus of the conversation, rather than the ideas and perspectives of the group.

Debrief as a group (15 minutes)

Get a group discussion going by asking the sub-groups to share their thoughts on the questions in the worksheet. Move between the groups so no single group gives all the answers. For example, if you have three groups ask question one to group A, question two to group B and question three to group C. Once each group has answered, check if any of the other groups have a different opinion.

There are no right or wrong responses in terms of actions to take. Discuss the merits of different courses of action. Even if someone says 'do nothing' it's good to discuss why –the pros and cons of that. It is important to role model inclusion and be non-judgemental in your facilitation.

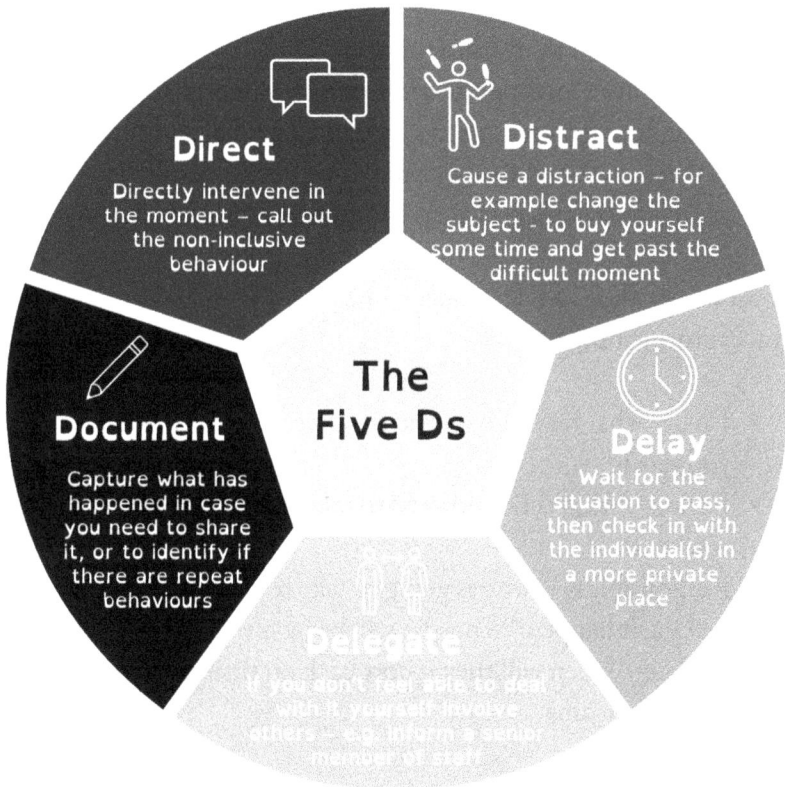

Direct
Directly intervene in the moment – call out the non-inclusive behaviour

Distract
Cause a distraction – for example change the subject - to buy yourself some time and get past the difficult moment

Document
Capture what has happened in case you need to share it, or to identify if there are repeat behaviours

The Five Ds

Delay
Wait for the situation to pass, then check in with the individual(s) in a more private place

Delegate
If you don't feel able to deal with it yourself involve others – e.g. inform a senior member of staff

Get a discussion going about inclusive language, banter and challenging non-inclusive behaviours (including what stops us challenging, and how difficult/easy it is to challenge in your team). You can use the Five Ds model to explore different ways of dealing with the situation.

You may want to introduce the concept of micro-behaviours (see the Respect chapter for more information) in the debrief.

Once you've gone through all the questions, ask these questions to bring the session to a close with some clear learning and actions for the team:

- What did you learn from this session?
- How can we incorporate what we've learnt to make our team more inclusive (as individuals and collectively)?
- Is there anything you'd like to see me do differently (if you are the team leader) to help with this?

You can use the GARU model to help you plan and ensure that you capture actions:

- Goal – what have you decided needs to be done? What is your goal?
- Action – what action(s) need to take place in order to achieve this?
- Responsibility – who is going to take responsibility for making it happen? Who else will be involved?
- Update – when will they report back on their progress to the wider team?

Keep the Momentum Going

The topic of inclusive language often comes up in this exercise: you may want to create an inclusive language guide for your team (see references for ideas).

It can be helpful to practise challenging non-inclusive behaviour through role-play. You can use the Five Ds model as a structure for role-playing different ways to challenge.

REFERENCES

A beginner's guide to pronouns and using pronouns in the workplace - Stonewall - https://www.stonewall.org.uk/workplace-trans-inclusion-hub/beginner%E2%80%99s-guide-pronouns-and-using-pronouns-workplace

Microaggressions YouTube Video - https://youtu.be/hDd3bzA7450

People Like Me Don't Belong Here: Identity Concealment is Associated with Negative Workplace Experiences - Journal of Social Issues (Reiman, Baretto & Tiemersma, 2017) - https://www.researchgate.net/publication/317950949_People_Like_Me_Don't_Belong_Here_Identity_Concealment_is_Associated_with_Negative_Workplace_Experiences

Say This, Not That: A Guide for Inclusive Language - The Diversity Movement - https://thediversitymovement.com/say-this-not-that-a-guide-for-inclusive-language/

The 5 Ds of Bystander Intervention - https://righttobe.org/guides/bystander-intervention-training/

The Inclusive Language Handbook – A Guide to Better Communication and Transformational Leadership - The Diversity Movement - https://theinclusivelanguagehandbook.com/

The Secret Resume Podcast Episode 12 - https://www.podbean.com/ew/pb-7rbhd-1418d2f

What Happened To You? (Oprah Winfrey & Dr Bruce Perry, 2022) - https://amzn.to/3R5nUuC

You Can't Multitask, So Stop Trying - Harvard Business Review (Paul Atchley, 2010) - https://hbr.org/2010/12/you-cant-multitask-so-stop-tr

PART TWO

IMPLEMENTATION

"The best big idea is only going to be as good as its implementation."

— *JAY SAMIT*

INTRODUCTION TO PART TWO

Part two of this book is about implementation. As this book is designed to be practical – to take and use immediately in your team, across your organisation, or with your clients – I thought it would be helpful to explore some of the ways you can use the model in an organisational context.

I have been consulting and facilitating for a long time, and I want to share with you some of the things I have learnt about working with teams, having conversations about DEI, and creating inclusive cultures in organisations.

This introduction shares three distinct ways of using the model. They can be used alone, adapted, or combined – feel free to be as innovative as you like!

Chapter Six looks at working at a team level – how to prepare yourself, how to facilitate DEI conversations, and some thoughts on dealing with resistance.

Chapter Seven touches on DEI strategy, and some of the other aspects of DEI that need to be in place if you want to have an organisation level/culture change impact.

If you're using the model just with a single team, Chapter Six will be most relevant to you. If you're looking at a more organisation-wide or systemic application, both chapters will be valuable.

This book comes with downloadable instructions and handouts for all the exercises in the book. They are available via the link at the back of the book. You have everything there that you need to start using the model and building your inclusive high performing team.

If you want to deepen your learning and access additional exercises and materials, I have developed an online course for DEI, L&D

and team development professionals, which will support you in using the model with a range of teams. The course is accompanied by a series of resources, including PowerPoint decks, a large bank of exercises and handouts, sample agendas and materials that will help you market and sell the approach to clients. I have also developed an online in-depth The Inclusive Team™ diagnostic that is available to those who have completed the online training and want to use this model across organisations or with multiple teams. Check out this link for further information.

https://liberareconsulting.co.uk/the-inclusive-team-programme

THREE APPROACHES TO IMPLEMENTATION

The Inclusive Team™ model can be used at all levels in an organisation from a single individual team all the way up to an organisation-wide initiative. Outlined below are some of the ways it can be used.

Option One: Intact Team Approach

When I talk about an intact team, I mean a real team that works towards a collective goal (see the Introduction to Part One for the difference between a team and a work group). This can be a permanent team, a matrixed team or a temporary project team – it doesn't matter. You can of course use the model and exercises with a work group; however, some of the questions and exercises may be less relevant because they are less important or do not apply as easily to a work group.

The model and exercises can be used as part of a team building away-day – form an agenda by combining different exercises that tackle the most challenging clusters or sub-clusters for your team. As an alternative you could integrate individual exercises into regular team meetings. For instance, if the team have a regular monthly meeting, time could be given each month for one The Inclusive Team™ exercise.

A team workshop can be facilitated by the team leader, a team member or by a third-party facilitator (internal DEI or L&D expert or an external consultant). You will find more detail and example agendas in Chapter Six.

Option Two: The Inclusive Team™ Workshops

The model and exercises can be used in a The Inclusive Team™ workshop made available to team leaders or team members from across the organisation. This is more of a training intervention, where you inspire the participants to develop their team to be inclusive and high performing, then provide them with materials to take back and work on with their own team. The agenda is typically an introduction to the model, practice with a couple of the exercises, then advice on implementation and facilitation. See Chapter Seven for an example.

This works very effectively when the participants are all team leaders and it is part of an organisation-wide initiative to create an inclusive culture: you teach the team leaders, and they return to their teams and use the materials to work on building inclusion at a team level.

However, it is also interesting to offer this workshop to all employees, particularly if attendance is on a voluntary basis. This allows you to identify individuals with a particular interest in inclusion who can become your inclusion champions across the organisation.

You may also have groups of key influencers who would benefit from the training and who play a key role in your DEI strategy. For instance, you could use a workshop like this with your Employee Resource Group leaders. The aim would be to develop their understanding of inclusion, and to equip them to use the model with their network leadership teams. This could be the first step in introducing the concept of inclusive teams to a broader audience in the organisation.

Option Three: Devolved Organisation-wide

This approach tends to work best when you use The Inclusive Team™ as a core element in your efforts to build an inclusive culture and where you want to roll it out across the whole organisation in a systemic way as a culture change initiative. It can be the most cost-effective method as no external facilitation is required, but don't underestimate the effort and drive an approach like this takes.

Note that it can also be done at a departmental or divisional level: it doesn't have to involve the whole organisation.

I like to use the Agile terminology of sprints for this approach. You create eight sprints, each a week or two long. An introductory sprint sets them up for success (when you introduce the approach and get the teams to complete the questionnaire handout), a week when they complete an exercise that helps build their personal business case for building an inclusive high performing team, one sprint per cluster (five in total), and then a closing sprint so that teams can integrate what they have learnt and create clear action plans. An example process is given in Chapter Seven.

The purpose of taking this approach is to create a strong momentum and shared language of inclusion across the organisation. It's not for the faint-hearted, and takes determination, drive, and strong stakeholder management – in particular it is essential to have support from the very top of the organisation. We will cover more on this in Chapter Seven.

CHAPTER 6

TEAM IMPLEMENTATION

"Be willing to be uncomfortable. Be comfortable being
uncomfortable."

— PETER MCWILLIAMS

This chapter focuses on using the model with an individual team,
either as part of a team building workshop or when using the exercises as part of weekly meetings. It is written primarily for a team
leader who wants to use the model and exercises with their team.

The information is also relevant if you are not the team leader or
are choosing an organisation-wide approach, as it covers topics
such as the practicalities (including some example agendas), facilitation tips and dealing with resistance. However, if you are thinking
of a more organisation-wide or broader application, you may want
to skip to Chapter Seven to get the bigger picture, and then return
to this chapter when you think about things in more practical
detail.

If you are not the team leader but are going to be facilitating the exercises, you will need to discuss much of what is written here with the leader to ensure you are aligned in the messaging and approach.

PRACTICALITIES

These are some of the things to consider when using the exercises as part of a team away-day or when adding a different exercise each time to your regular team catch up.

The exercises I have shared each last about 45-60 minutes, though you can adjust the time to fit in with your agenda. Just make sure you give enough time for people to have a good conversation – there is no point in a superficial conversation where nothing of consequence is discussed.

When using with your team, start by getting the team members to respond to the ten questions in the 'Team Survey' handout in the downloadable materials that accompany the book. The link is on the last page of the book. They can do this anonymously – they don't have to put their names on their question sheets. Collect in the answers and work out an average for each cluster and sub-cluster so you can identify your highest and lowest scoring areas.

You can then choose the appropriate exercises that will develop the clusters or sub-clusters you are most concerned about. This book contains one exercise per sub-cluster. You may choose to only focus on these areas, or to gradually work through all ten exercises over time.

Team take 10 question survey

↓

Average results & decide focus areas

↓

Design team development based on focus areas

Team Away-Day   or   Integrate into regular team meetings

Evaluate

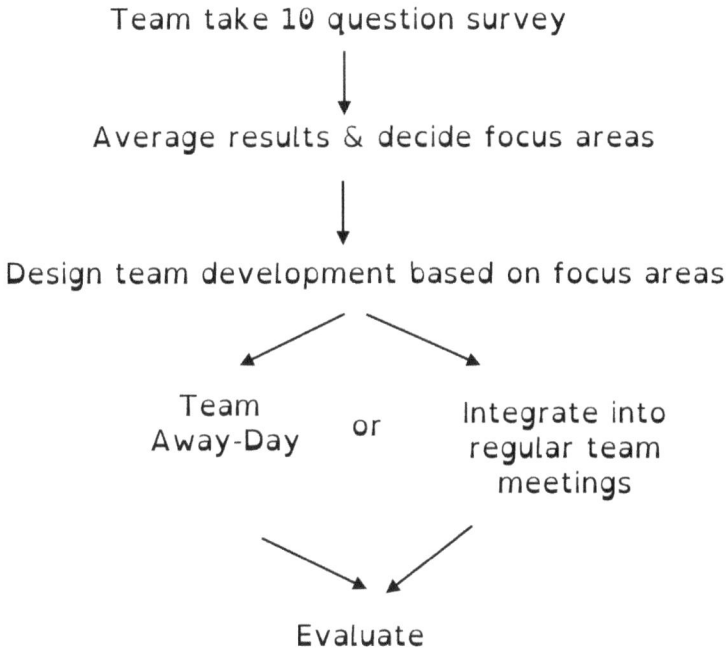

The process would look something like this:

It is important to set yourself and the team up for success. Diving straight into an exercise may feel uncomfortable for the team, they are unlikely to open up and you may get strong resistance (see more on that later in the chapter).

Therefore, take time to plan carefully how you are going to introduce The Inclusive Team™ approach to your team. I recommend first taking some time to reflect on why you think it is important to you, your team and the organisation. In other words, identify your personal perspective on the business case for the team. You may need to ask yourself some difficult questions about why this is important to you and challenge yourself on some perceptions and assumptions you have. I have included a worksheet to help you do that in the materials that accompany this book.

You can share this perspective with the team to explain why you believe it is important for you collectively to work on becoming a more inclusive high performing team.

Before diving into the exercises from the model, I also recommend an initial exercise where each team member works out their own personal business case for creating an inclusive high performing team (you can use the same handout mentioned above). This can be a great motivator. It helps team members to connect to their own 'why' and helps them identify what is in it for them. Remember, you are trying to encourage behaviour change from team members and supporting them to connect to their own 'why' is very helpful in creating momentum for change. The section on resistance later in this chapter helps explain why this part of the process is important.

Below are two example agendas – the first for a one-day workshop and the second taking the approach of working through one exercise a week. Both examples assume the team have taken the ten-question survey and that you have identified five sub-clusters as the areas where you want to focus. They also both give time for the team members to connect to their own 'why' (as mentioned above).

Example Full Day Team Workshop Agenda	
Introduction – Share own business case and results of diagnostic. Introductions if team don't know each other well.	- 45 mins
Build momentum for change - My business case exercise – helps get team members engaged in creating a more inclusive team	- 45 mins
Alignment – Direction exercise	- 50 mins
Break	- 10 mins
Adaptability – Flexibility exercise	- 50 mins
Lunch	- 50 mins
Respect – Diversity exercise	- 50 mins
Trust – Conflict exercise	- 45 mins
Break	- 10 mins
Growth – Improvement exercise	- 50 mins
Action planning , Next Steps & close	- 45 mins

The workshop approach allows you to work quickly and discuss a number of related topics in a short period of time. This means that the conversations can get quite deep quite fast.

One challenge is that the exercises have all been designed to have pre-work that is completed before the exercise is delivered. You may want to ask the team to do some of the pre-work beforehand, and then include some of the pre-work as an activity on the day so you don't overload the team with work to do before the workshop. The exercise instructions and handouts are all available as downloads and they include additional suggestions if you want to do the exercises without any pre-work or include the pre-work in the exercise.

Example Weekly Team Agenda	
Introduction – Share own business case and results of diagnostic.	Week 1
Build momentum for change - My business case exercise – helps get team members engaged in creating a more inclusive team	Week 2
Alignment – Direction exercise	Week 3
Adaptability – Flexibility exercise	Week 4
Respect – Diversity exercise	Week 5
Trust – Conflict exercise	Week 6
Growth – Improvement exercise	Week 7
Action planning & Next Steps	Week 8

The weekly approach allows the team members to absorb the information and apply the learning more slowly, and gives them plenty of time to complete the pre-work.

Note that you design your own agenda by including the exercises on which you want to focus in your team development. Make sure you give thought to the order of the exercises and flow of the agenda. For instance, after the introductory and building momentum sections I started with an exercise on team purpose (Direction exercise) then one analysing the system in which the team operates (Flexibility exercise). These are relatively safe topics and allow the team to warm up and get used to working together in this way.

I then move on to some of the more inter-personally challenging exercises such as the Diversity and Conflict exercises. I finish with the Improvement exercise which is where team members discuss their greatest mistakes. I chose to put this exercise last as it requires the participants to be open and vulnerable, and the previous exercises will have warmed them up for that. It can also be quite fun as there is an opportunity to award a prize; thus it can be a good, positive final exercise.

The exercises are designed so they can be facilitated by the team leader, a member of the team, or an external facilitator. If you are doing it for yourself, the following section gives you some advice about effective facilitation of team development and DEI conversations. They are not always easy discussions, so it is important to prepare yourself well, and you may want to consider having a neutral third party to facilitate, particularly if you are including the exercises in an away-day where the cumulative effect of multiple exercises on the topic means the team is likely to get into some deeper discussions.

FACILITATION

Let's not pretend that facilitating discussions about diversity, inclusion and team high performance is always straightforward. In particular, the conversation around DEI seems to have become increasingly polarised lately, with accusations, blame and provocative language being used which inflames and makes people defensive, rather than moving the conversation forward.

Here are some of my top tips for facilitating potentially challenging conversations.

Preparation

- Prepare yourself – make sure you've read all the instructions carefully and understand how to facilitate the exercise. This may seem obvious, but the more comfortable you are with the flow of the exercise the smoother it will run.

- Read the chapter of the book that the exercise relates to and spend time reflecting on what messages you want to convey. Think about areas of resistance you might encounter.

- Be optimistic – don't assume the conversation will always be difficult! That may seem counter to what I've just said, but the times in my career I've been expecting the most resistance and push back have *not* been the most difficult conversations.

- Share information beforehand so that people have time to think – not everybody likes to think on their feet. Most of the exercises come with some pre-work to prepare the team for the discussion.

- If you are anxious, do some breathing exercises to help calm your nervous system. I find 4:8 breathing, where you breathe in for a count of four and out for a count of eight, really helps me calm my nervous system.

- If possible, set up the room with chairs in a circle – this helps facilitate a conversation. If you're doing this virtually, encourage the team to have their cameras on. Everyone being able to read each other's body language and facial expressions really helps. You may have people in your team who have a strong preference for having their camera off for all or some of the time. For example, some people who are neurodivergent find that camera on all the time is really difficult for them. Make sure you talk to them in advance and agree a solution and the best way to ensure they are able to fully contribute. This also applies to people who are often quiet in your team meetings. Try to have some time with them beforehand to encourage them to speak up in the session, and/or to work out a way for them to contribute more.

- Make sure you have space for breakout conversations so people can have a conversation without being overheard. If you are using video conferencing, ensure you know how to use breakout rooms. Many of the exercises break the group into sub-groups for at least some of the time.
- You don't have to identify sub-groups before a session, but if you have line reporting relationships in the group you might want to ensure the line manager and direct report aren't in the same sub-group. Or you might want to ensure that the sub-groups are a mixture of people who know each other less well or work together less frequently. If you are doing multiple exercises, get people to move around between groups so they are working with and getting to know different people.

During the exercise/workshop

You are trying to create an inclusive and safe space where people are able to express their point of view, even if it is contrary to what others think. You can revisit the Psychological Safety section in the Trust chapter to refresh yourself on this. This may be the first time that team members have been encouraged to openly discuss certain sensitive topics.

Start as you mean to go on:

- Start the conversation with a discussion about why you are doing this – why it is important to you and the team.
- Establish inclusive team norms for behaviour during the activity/workshop. This step is often skipped, but it is really important to help the exercise run well. I find it helpful to ask the group to shout out ideas for group

behaviours that will make the session most effective (e.g. confidentiality, respect each other's ideas, listen to each other, everyone to contribute, it's ok to disagree, etc.). I capture this on a flip chart (or electronically if doing this virtually) and give it a name such as 'team charter' or 'ground rules'. You can use it as a reminder by drawing the group's attention to it if you feel things are going off course. Something simple like, "Shall we check in and see if we are keeping to the team charter?" can be a helpful way of getting people to step back from the discussion and reflect on their behaviour. If you are running multiple sessions, you can keep the list and review it at the beginning of each session.

Keep in mind:

- Don't think that you need to have all the answers: keep throwing the conversation back to the group. This isn't a conversation between you and the group; you are not supposed to be the expert on the topic, you are facilitating a conversation between the whole group. I find phrases like, "What does everyone else think?" or, "Does anyone else have a view on that?" really help. This is a key difference between facilitation and training.
- Be aware of power dynamics, particularly if you are the team leader. Your position can mean people automatically place additional weight on what you have to say, so be careful to keep your contributions to a minimum or keep what you have to say until later in the conversation.
- Try to keep calm, even if others are having strong emotions. Remember the 4:8 breathing technique I mentioned above.

- Remind yourself that disagreement and conflict are ok, and there is no right answer!
- It is ok to take a break if things get heated or if you want to have a one-to-one discussion with someone. Sometimes it is better to talk to someone alone than tackle them in front of the group. Take a look at the Five Ds model in the Respect chapter for more information on ways to deal with challenging behaviour.

Inclusive facilitation:

Try to role model inclusive behaviours in the way you facilitate the workshop. For example:

- Inclusion is about everybody present having a voice. Make sure you establish that as an expectation upfront and invite everyone to contribute. Look out for people who are not saying much and ask if they have something to say. Design the workshop/activity so people can contribute in different ways (large group/small group/pairs/individual work) to recognise that not everyone enjoys or is comfortable speaking in front of a large group.
- Look out for people who are talking a lot and not giving space for other quieter members to speak. Perhaps they are speaking over others. My personal preference is to tackle it gently at first and if they do not take the hint then be more direct! This can be an example of when a quiet word away from the rest of the group allows someone to receive feedback and save face.
- Respect everybody's point of view. This can be the most difficult. I find repeating Carl Rogers' phrase 'unconditional positive regard' in my head helpful if

someone says something I find difficult or strongly disagree with. Rogers was a psychologist and said the term meant that you should respect others and give them permission to have their own feelings and experiences. You can of course put forward a different perspective – after all, the purpose of the exercises is to hear different points of view – but it doesn't mean that just because somebody has a point of view you don't agree with or you find unacceptable, they are wrong and you are right, or that you should shut them down. See the 'Everyone is entitled to their opinion' section below for more on this.

- Watch your language. This is a personal preference, and I know some DEI practitioners will disagree with me, but I recommend avoiding using potentially inflammatory words or phrases such as 'white privilege' or 'white fragility' (see references if you want to know more about those terms). For instance, you can talk about 'Headwinds and Tailwinds' (see the Respect chapter for more on this) without talking about white privilege. You can recognise or observe that someone is feeling/being defensive without using the phrase 'white fragility'. You can talk about majorities and minorities without denigrating white middle-aged men. I once heard a story of how someone said to their clients (a group of senior, white, middle-aged men), "What does it feel like to be an endangered species?" These conversations can be difficult enough without using phrases that immediately make people feel defensive. Nobody is going to come round to your perspective if you make them feel on the back foot and bad about themselves. Building an inclusive culture is hard work and it needs people in majority groups to be allies and involved in the solution – they are unlikely to do that if you alienate them and make them feel defensive.

- Know yourself. Understanding your own inclusive behaviours, your tolerance for conflict and expression of emotion is incredibly important. For example, some coaches and facilitators I have met are uncomfortable if someone cries. That has never bothered me, but I have previously struggled when people express overt anger, because I come from a family where we typically didn't do that. Lots of personal development and my training as a trauma practitioner have helped me overcome that, but I know that in the past I may have not given people I was working with the space to express their anger because it made me uncomfortable.

DEALING WITH RESISTANCE

It is almost inevitable that you will encounter resistance at some point. Either vocal, active resistance or quieter, perhaps more passive-aggressive activity. This chapter talks about resistance in workshops or training, and then Chapter Seven looks at it from a more systemic perspective where careful application of change management practices will help minimise the potential of resistance from across the system.

A wise person once told me: 'Resistance is a source of information, not something to be overcome'. I can't find a source for the quote, but it's always stuck with me. It is easy to go into convincing over-drive when you encounter someone with strong opinions who seems determined to derail something... to shower them with reasons why they should change their mind and move over to your more enlightened path! If we see their resistance as their way of trying to tell us something it allows us to move into a more curious mindset.

Resistance can be overt, when someone vocally disagrees, or covert, when the individual tells you by their behaviour that they don't agree – they may be there in person but completely disengaged, e.g. multi-tasking, or perhaps not turning up to meetings at all.

I try to remember a couple of things when dealing with any kind of resistance:

Everybody is entitled to their opinion

We can expect certain behaviours from team members, but we cannot control their minds. I saw a post on LinkedIn recently that stated that 'agree to disagree' has no place in DEI. The author and I will have to agree to disagree with that perspective, and it is an example of the polarising, binary thinking that maintains the status quo. Not everybody has to think the same. We can agree to disagree. People can change their minds. Agreeing to disagree means that for the moment you recognise you are coming from a different perspective, and that's ok. Sometimes you have to move on from a conversation. It might not be comfortable, but that's ok. One of you might change your mind in the future. Maybe you won't. And that's ok too.

This isn't to say that any behaviour is acceptable, or that you shouldn't step in if you notice that someone is feeling hurt and upset by another's views. It is absolutely reasonable for a team/leader to articulate behavioural norms such as respect and expect the team to adhere to them. It does mean that I believe it is unhelpful to always shut down dissenting voices just because they make the discussion uncomfortable. One essential element of building an inclusive team is that the team and the facilitator become comfortable with being uncomfortable, and that they learn that difficult and emotional topics can be discussed without it descending into shouting, insults or angry exchanges.

Remember that the exercises are an opportunity for the team to practise working together in an inclusive way – to learn how to access their collective intelligence. If somebody is dominating, find a way to get others to speak so you can hear more voices and perspectives.

It is also worth bearing in mind that the learning doesn't all have to take place in the group. For instance, if a team member is upsetting others – perhaps completely unintentionally –having a quiet one-to-one with them to help them understand their impact is likely to be more powerful than calling them out in the group and embarrassing them. Take a look at the Five Ds that we covered in the chapter on Respect for more on ways of challenging inappropriate behaviour.

You are asking people to change their behaviour, and change is hard!

We are all in a different place on our DEI journey, which means that how you need to behave in order to help them is different. A long time ago I read the book *Changing for Good* by James O Prochaska, and it completely altered my perspective on how people change, and how to help people along their transformation journey. It had a profound effect on how I do my job.

Stage	What You See	How To Help
Pre-contemplation	Deflection, Humour, Clever arguments, Rationalisation, Denial, Staying in their head, Projection, Wanting to change others rather than themselves.	Helping them see the impact of their behaviour. Don't push too hard for them to either acknowledge the problem or to take action - they will dig in their heels even more.
Contemplation	Soul searching, Honesty, Finding out information. Curiosity. Open to challenge. Reflection. Dreaming, Visioning - what will it look like when I get there?	Empathy, Supportive warmth. Helpful information (e.g. where/how to find out more). Education. Sharing a vision. Don't push too hard to take action – they are not ready yet.
Preparation	Goal Setting. Planning what, how, where, when.	Supporting in the way they want you to. Help with planning/preparation.
Action	Taking action, changing behaviour.	Reward and give positive feedback for new behaviours. Contract your roles.
Maintenance	Maintaining helpful behaviours.	Revise contract – confront if slipping back into old ways.

Adapted from 'Changing for Good' by James Prochaska et al

One of the key messages I took from the book was that people go through several phases before they take any action to change. You can see my interpretation of the phases in the table below. Note that the process is not linear – in fact Prochaska draws it as a spiral – and people often move back and forth between the stages.

I hadn't previously given much thought to 'pre-contemplation'. This is when someone is not really thinking much about the topic – they do not want to engage. They are just not ready yet. Typical behaviours from someone at this point are arguing or avoiding a topic – both are ways of avoiding the cognitive dissonance that occurs when information comes in that is contrary to what you believe (see the Alignment chapter for more on cognitive dissonance). You might see someone vociferously defending or denying a certain perspective (for example, "We don't have a problem with racism in the UK; it's not like the US," or, "We're pretty inclusive here already; we have a meritocracy and anyone can succeed.") Perhaps they are avoiding it (for example, disengaging from the conversation, or making other things a priority, so that they don't turn up to meetings).

Researchers at Harvard suggest these behaviours are a result of feeling threat (something we've discussed in most of the chapters in this book), either threat to status (thinking it's a zero-sum game – if minority groups get more then majority groups will get less, and they might personally be impacted), or a threat to self-image – perhaps they see themselves as a 'good' and 'moral' person so find it difficult to accept they may be doing anything that might be 'bad', such as having biases. Alternatively, they may perceive a threat to their self-image of succeeding on their own terms. If they acknowledge that the workplace isn't a meritocracy and that structural inequities may have held some groups back, what does that say about their success, which they have been led to believe is down to their hard work, talent and determination?

The stinger here is that if you try to push someone who is in precontemplation, they will become increasingly resistant and dig their heels in more. This can feel really difficult, particularly if you are deeply passionate about creating a more inclusive team.

My favourite saying when it comes to change is 'don't try to push water uphill'. What I mean by this is that there is no point expending your energy trying to convince people in the precontemplation stage that they should get on board. Focus your energy and effort on those who are already part way there and work to create a momentum that will bring others along in its wake.

This doesn't mean completely ignoring those who initially appear to be at an earlier stage in their journey, particularly if they demonstrate a degree of curiosity. I remember one CEO I worked with who was a very straight-talking man. I was working with his top team, and they collectively were right at the beginning of their DEI journey. They didn't have a strategy and had done very little to create a more diverse or inclusive organisation. During the day-long workshop he and I had a number of frank exchanges in which I directly challenged his thinking on a couple of topics. One was the employment of disabled people in his organisation *('I would never employ a disabled person in that role'),* and another was his use of banter in the top team *('I want it to be fun to work here'* or *'He doesn't mind if I make comments about him being Jewish; he knows it's only a joke').*

The CEO stated his opinions pretty directly and forcefully, and it might have been easy to assume that he was in the pre-contemplation stage. However, he had been very clear at the beginning of the workshop that he wanted the team to be challenged, so I took him at his word and tackled his comments head on. I found that he was actually open to being disagreed with; in fact, I think he quite enjoyed it. I'm not saying he suddenly became a changed man, but I do know that because I presented a different perspective in a respectful but direct way, he changed his mind, particularly on the topic of disabled employees.

I had initially put a toe in the water by openly disagreeing with him, and once I saw he was open to challenge I could see he was in the contemplation stage: he was trying to gather information and was open to being educated and his views being tested.

Sometimes mindset follows behaviours

We tend to believe that we have to change somebody's mind in order for them to behave in a particular way – so we need to convince someone of the benefits of DEI before they will behave in an inclusive manner. However, research has shown that it can be the other way around. If we create an expectation of inclusive behaviours in the team, and the team hold each other accountable for those behaviours, over time mindsets may change as people see the benefits of inclusion and alter their perspective.

I think of inclusion as having three core elements – mindset, knowledge and behaviours. We often focus on using knowledge to improve mindset and therefore behaviours, but it doesn't have to be that way. In truth, they are all interrelated, and you can start with any one of the three and still have an impact on the other two.

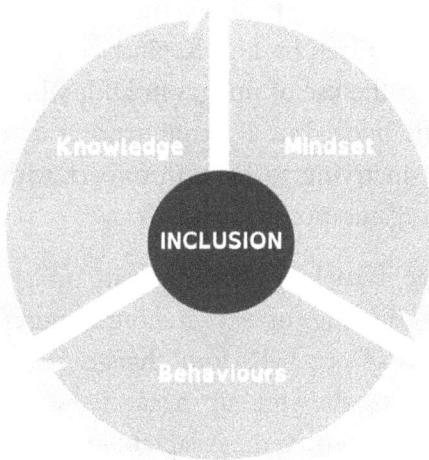

I came across some fascinating research that found that when people were asked to nod their heads whilst reading arguments for or against university tuition increases, they ended up agreeing with the arguments more than if they didn't nod their head. Their behaviour influenced their mindset.

You may have heard of something called 'nudge theory', created by Richard Thaler and Cass Sunstein and made famous (or should I say infamous) here in the UK by the Government's Behavioural Insights Team – also known as the 'Nudge Unit' which was set up to apply behavioural science to public policy. The team used a rigorous approach of experimentation with nudges to see if they could encourage citizens to behave differently in a broad range of ways. For instance, they helped the courts service increase the number of fine payments made by using personalised text message prompts. They also found that by telling people who were late paying their taxes that most people in their town had already paid, payment rates increased by about fifteen percent.

The idea behind nudges is that you can get people to change their behaviour without needing to argue, threaten or punish. There is an excellent book written by Lisa Kepinski and Tinna C Nielsen (see references) on the use of nudges in DEI, which is far beyond the scope of this book, but I recommend as a 'must read' for anyone involved in trying to have an impact with diversity and inclusion on an organisation-wide scale.

The key message I took is that you can nudge or encourage behaviour in a broad range of ways and our mindset or beliefs may change as a result of our behaviour change. It is our old friend cognitive dissonance showing up again (you can refresh your memory on that by revisiting the Adaptability chapter). Our minds don't like inconsistency, so if our behaviour has changed, the cognitive dissonance we feel means we need to change our minds to align with our behaviours.

INTELLECTUAL HUMILITY AND DIALOGUE

In his excellent book *Difficult Conversations*, Douglas Stone says, "People almost never change without first feeling understood." The desire to convince, persuade and be right gets in the way of us seeking to truly understand the perspective of someone with a different view from our own. This can be particularly true regarding topics such as diversity and inclusion because they are so closely tied to our values.

I mentioned the concept of Intellectual Humility in the Adaptability chapter, and I find it is particularly useful to bear in mind both from the personal perspective of facilitating a discussion, and as something to be encouraged in an inclusive team.

When someone comes from a perspective of intellectual humility, they are able to talk more dispassionately about ideas because they have separated the ideas from themselves (or more accurately from their ego), and are therefore less attached to them. They respect others' views and are willing to revise their own.

To me this naturally links to the concept of dialogue, which I believe is a significant but over-looked practice that could have a massive impact on DEI in organisations and indeed society.

Much of what we do in teams is debate: we put forward our perspectives in the hope that *others* will learn, change, and grow. When we enter into dialogue, we do so in order that *we* can learn, change, and grow. The goal in debate is to win; the goal in dialogue is to listen and gain a deeper understanding.

My friend Gen recently shared a poem by the Sufi mystic Rumi, and I was particularly struck by the first line: 'Out beyond ideas of wrongdoing and rightdoing, there is a field. I'll meet you there.' For me this captures the essence of dialogue: the ability to talk and connect in a way that is beyond judgement.

It is a complex topic, and I won't pretend that introducing dialogue in organisations is easy. But I do believe that developing our dialogue skills plays a part if we want to create a truly inclusive team or organisation. I have included some references at the end of this chapter so you can explore the topic in more depth if you wish.

Reducing Threat

Being detached from our ideas, listening hard and talking dispassionately about topics that are close to our values can be difficult if you feel threatened in the ways described by the Harvard researchers I mentioned earlier. They suggest a number of ways of reducing the threat so that people can engage more readily in discussions about inclusion.

They propose helping people shift from the perspective that it is a zero-sum game to one that inclusion is good for everyone. In addition to the idea that feeling included is important to everyone, there are some great practical examples of where something that was designed to ensure equity for a minority group has also been helpful for people in the majority.

For instance, dropped kerbs or automatic door openers were originally installed to help people with disabilities, and are also incredibly helpful to people with prams, bikes or suitcases. Or how about the blurred background feature on your Zoom or Teams call that helps you present a professional image and hide your messy room (or is that just me?): did you know it was originally introduced by Microsoft to help people who are deaf or hard of hearing to lipread because it keeps the focus on the speaker.

A client of mine has highlighted the 'inclusion is for everyone' message in their organisation by creating a DEI strategy with the tagline: *'Enabling a culture that values difference and delivers fairness for all'*. The statement is a positive one that people can move towards, and highlights that inclusion is for everyone, not just under-represented groups. The exercise I have suggested for the Diversity sub-cluster in the Respect chapter is also a helpful way for everyone to connect to their own diversity and feelings of exclusion, which helps them recognise that inclusion is for them even if they are not in an under-represented group.

The second suggestion is to bolster self-esteem so that the threat to self-identity is minimised. It is almost like self-esteem creates a cushion against threats to self-identity. I have captured a simplified example of this below:

Belief

The world is fair and people succeed on their own merit

Self Image

I have skills and talent and succeeded on my own hard work and merit

Alternative belief

The world isn't fair and there are structural biases that prevent some people from succeeding

High self esteem

If I believe this then maybe my hard work and merit weren't the only reasons why I succeeded, and that's ok.

Updates self image and original belief

Low self esteem

If I believe this then maybe my hard work and merit weren't the only reasons why I succeeded. So who am I?

Too threatening to self image so defends original belief

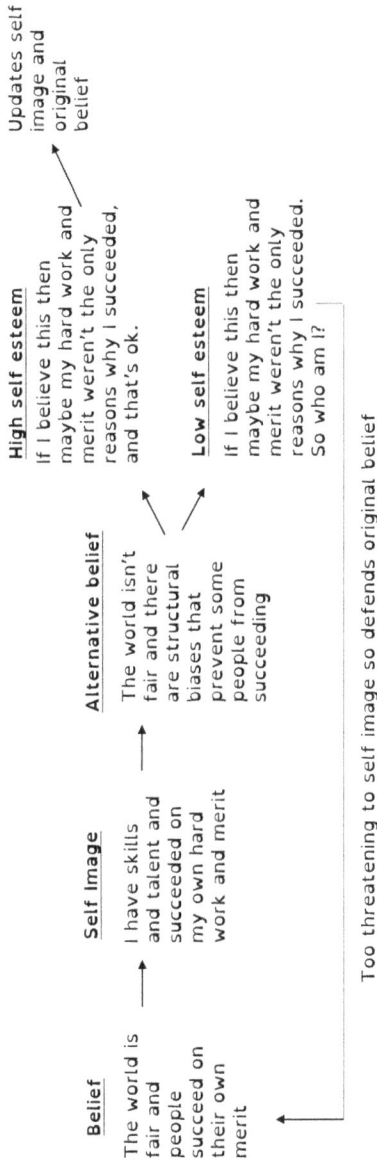

This gives rise to the suggestion that rather than beginning a workshop with data and facts that may have the effect of increasing the self-image threat (which I have frequently seen happen), we should

start with something that helps build self-esteem. This boost to self-esteem doesn't have to be related to the topic – a general increase in self-esteem is enough to lessen the need to respond in a biased or defensive manner. This could be as simple as asking everyone at the beginning of a workshop or meeting to share something that went well for them or they are proud of that week. An example of a self-esteem building exercise is included in the downloads that accompany this book.

The final suggestion the researchers make is to link DEI efforts to moral ideals rather than moral obligations, which is a subtle but important difference. Moral ideals are positive goals or aspirations that reflect our beliefs and values (such as equal treatment). Moral obligations are rules or duties we feel we must follow (such as non-discrimination). The way I think of it is that moral ideals are a choice and moral obligations are things we do because others/society tells us we should. By taking this approach we reduce the threat people feel to their self-image as a good or moral person by helping them connect behaviour change to their moral ideals. We are helping them move towards doing something positive (be inclusive) rather than away from something negative (don't be biased, don't discriminate). The activity of getting people to connect to their own business case that is included in downloads and part of the example agendas I have shared in this and the next chapter should help with this.

EVALUATION

The eagle eyed among you will notice that I included 'evaluate' in the exemplar process earlier in this chapter but haven't mentioned it since. Evaluation is an essential element of any team or organisational intervention, and I cover the topic extensively in the next chapter.

REFERENCES

Changing for Good (Prochaska, Norcross & DiClemente, 2007) - https://amzn.to/3R6gkA9

Dialogue: The Art Of Thinking Together (William Isaacs, 1999) - https://amzn.to/49L8Zgq

Difficult Conversations: How to Discuss What Matters Most (Stone, Patton & Heen, 2023) - https://amzn.to/3G7LpgA

Inclusion Nudges Guidebook (Lista Kepinski & Tinna C Nielsen, 2020) - https://amzn.to/3R3dVpI

Robin DiAngelo on "White Fragility" - YouTube Video - https://youtu.be/Qx-gUfQx4-Q

Speaking Together: Applying the principles and practice of dialogue (Alison Jones) - https://www.spaceforlearning.com/docs/Speaking%20Together%20-%20Alison%20Jones%20Sep%2007.pdf

To overcome resistance to DEI, understand what's driving it - Harvard Business Review (Shuman, Knowles & Goldenberg, 2023) - https://hbr.org/2023/03/to-overcome-resistance-to-dei-understand-whats-driving-it

What is White Privilege - BBC Bitesize - https://www.bbc.co.uk/bitesize/articles/zrvkbqt

CHAPTER 7

ORGANISATIONAL IMPLEMENTATION

"How do you eat an elephant? One bite at a time."

— *DESMOND TUTU*

In this chapter we will explore how The Inclusive Team™ model can be used to facilitate change at a broader departmental or organisational level – how it can help build a culture of inclusion and high performance that stretches far beyond that of an individual team.

This is the area that excites me most: the idea of building an inclusive culture one team at a time – or eating that elephant one bite at a time. This is about role modelling The Inclusive Team™ behaviours in your implementation process, by shifting the power and distributing responsibility for an inclusive culture to everyone in the organisation.

In this chapter I cover some of the implementation practicalities of using the model at an organisational level and how it is important to use a systemic lens to design DEI strategy and initiatives. Finally,

I will share some of the lessons I have learnt about change management, including how resistance shows up at an organisational level.

PRACTICALITIES

In the introduction to Part Two I gave two examples of how the model can be used at an organisational level. The first is in The Inclusive Team™ workshops that are made available to team leaders or team members, and the second is to create a devolved department or organisation-wide initiative where the model is adopted and used by the whole department/organisation in a series of coordinated activities. Additional detail is given about each approach below.

Option One: The Inclusive Team™ Workshop Approach

This is more aligned with a traditional training approach, where team leaders or team members attend a workshop – often with a mixed group of participants from different parts of the organisation – to learn about the model and how to facilitate the exercises with their team.

The criticism I have heard of many DEI training programmes is that they are not practical enough and participants struggle to transfer their learning to their day-to-day roles.

This approach differs in that the focus is less on the participants learning about themselves, and more on how they are going to apply their learning. It is a bit like a 'Train the Trainer' approach. There is an explicit expectation that they take action and apply their learning with their team after the workshop. To support them with this they are given the handouts that come as a download with this book which are designed with clear instructions for teams to use independently.

The Inclusive Team™ workshops can be stand alone or complementary to conscious inclusion/inclusive leadership training you may already have implemented.

This approach can be very effective in supporting team leaders to feel confident to have potentially difficult conversations with their teams, and you can use it as a way to ensure consistency and that core organisational messages are conveyed.

This method also works well with mixed groups of individuals. One client with a very matrixed project team structure is putting all their employees through The Inclusive Team™ training to ensure they all get the same information and learning. They will then go away and work in their teams to implement the exercises.

The process would look something like this:

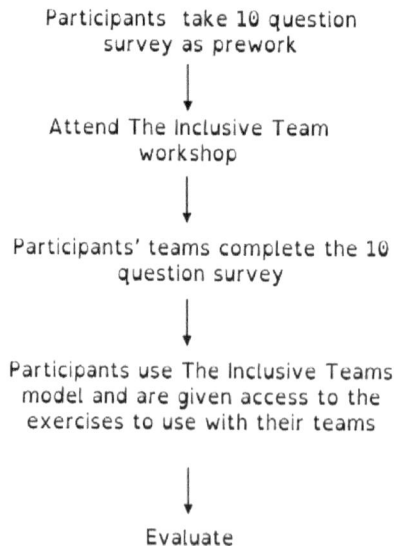

Participants take 10 question
survey as prework

↓

Attend The Inclusive Team
workshop

↓

Participants' teams complete the 10
question survey

↓

Participants use The Inclusive Teams
model and are given access to the
exercises to use with their teams

↓

Evaluate

Here is an exemplar workshop agenda. The first two sessions are about creating the right conditions for learning, building momentum for change and reducing potential for resistance. See Chapter Six for more information on this.

Example Half Day The Inclusive Team™ Workshop	
Introduction – Individual introductions, business case for Inclusive Teams, Introduction to the model	- 45mins
Build momentum for change - My business case exercise – helps get participants engaged in building inclusive teams	- 45 mins
Break	- 10 mins
Respect – Diversity exercise – to demonstrate how to facilitate an exercise	- 50 mins
Implementation – share process and discussion how to implement in their teams	- 45 mins
Action planning , Next Steps & close	- 45 mins

Option Two: Devolved Organisation-wide Approach

This approach is suitable when you have strong senior level buy-in and desire to rapidly build a more inclusive culture. It can be used at a departmental or organisation-wide level. It requires excellent communication, explicit senior level support and engagement, energy and drive, and trust in leaders to implement on a local level.

Benefits include building a sense of momentum, creation of a language for inclusion, and a strong message that creating an inclusive high performing team culture is important to your organisation and that it is everyone's responsibility. You are also role modelling aspects of The Inclusive Team™ model by delegating and trusting that teams will engage with the activity and own the implementation.

In this approach, the organisation designs a high-level framework with the expectation that every team will follow the same process over (for example) an eight-week period.

Each week there is a 'sprint' on a particular topic where a video or reading materials is made available to team leaders at the beginning of the week. This gives them background information and lets them know what they are expected to do that week. You also provide them with the materials they need to run the exercises with their team.

The team leaders then facilitate one of the exercises for that cluster with their team by the deadline (end of the week). Each week a new cluster is introduced until you have covered all five.

Below is an example of how this could work in practice. There are eight weeks in total as the first two are used to (a) introduce the concept/get the team to complete the ten-question survey (included in the downloads that accompany the book) and (b) build momentum for change by getting teams to connect to their own business case for building an inclusive high performing team. This is the same as in the other approaches I have shared and is about creating the right environment for change and reducing potential resistance – more detail can be found in Chapter Six. The final sprint (week eight) is there for extracting key learning and action planning.

Example Organisation Wide Approach	
Introduction – Share organisation's business case and the 8 week plan. Get teams to complete the 10 question handout	Week 1
Build momentum for change – Teams complete and discuss the My business case exercise – helps get team members engaged in creating a more inclusive team	Week 2
Alignment – teams choose between the Direction and Accountability exercises	Week 3
Adaptability – Teams choose between the Flexibility and Innovation exercises	Week 4
Respect – teams choose between the Diversity and Belonging exercises	Week 5
Trust – teams choose between the Empowerment and Conflict exercises	Week 6
Growth – teams choose between the Improvement and Development exercises	Week 7
Action planning & Next Steps	Week 8

To be effective and to implement real lasting change, both approaches I outline above require you to take a more systemic view of DEI and how it interacts with the organisational system.

SYSTEMIC DEI

The biggest mistake I see organisations make when trying to create a more inclusive high performing team culture is to implement a range of isolated tactical approaches that are not joined up or well thought through. Often, they are a knee-jerk response driven by a desire to move to rapid action and tend to be an implementation of something that has worked in another organisation.

I am sorry to say that mandating a half hour Unconscious Bias e-learning module for everyone, or setting up some employee networks with no governance, or running a couple of half day Inclusive Recruitment workshops just for the Talent Acquisition team isn't going to make much difference.

Successful organisations who are really moving the dial on DEI take a systemic, strategic approach. They understand why they are doing it, where they want to get to, what their specific challenges are, and the actions they are going to take. They recognise that creating an inclusive organisation is a culture change. Most importantly, they understand that they are operating in a system, and that they need to ensure the activities they implement are aligned with each other *and* to the DEI and organisational strategies.

By paying attention to the system and taking a Change Management approach, you will hugely reduce the potential for resistance to your inclusion initiative. That isn't to say you will never encounter opposition – you absolutely will, but you will also build positive momentum that will bring enough people with you to create a real change.

ALIGNED DEI

At Liberare Consulting we use the ABCD model (see below) to help our clients think through the different elements of creating an aligned strategic DEI plan. I have included a brief explanation of each element below.

The ABCD of Aligned DEI

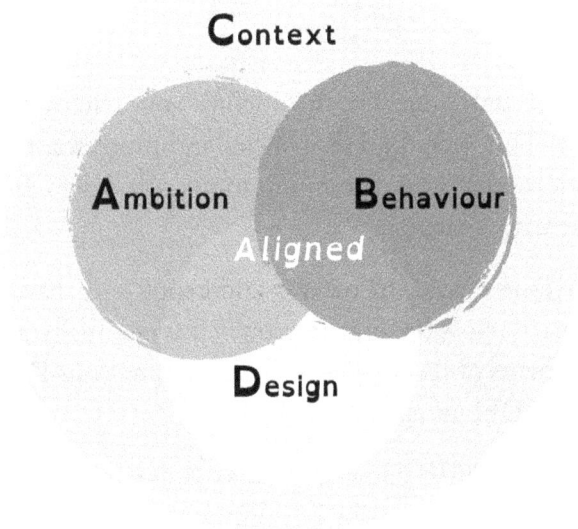

Ambition

A clearly articulated vision and strategy for DEI. This includes governance structures, targets, KPIs, top team commitment and sponsorship and clear DEI accountability throughout the organisation.

Behaviour

Individual and collective behaviours that create a diverse and inclusive culture. This includes a definition of expected behaviours, training and development, and senior leadership role modelling of inclusive behaviours.

Context

The internal and external context that influence the speed and ease of change. This includes things like the organisation's culture, other competing or complementary initiatives, diversity of talent in the sector and country legislation/targets.

Design

The systems and processes that define and reinforce inclusive behaviours. This includes HR policies and processes, reward and recognition mechanisms, communications, job design and change management approaches.

If you genuinely want to make a difference – to have real and lasting impact across the organisation – it is essential you consider all four elements of this model when developing your DEI strategy and planning DEI initiatives.

The Inclusive Team™ allows you to work at a team level to build an inclusive culture from the bottom up. It fits in the *Behaviour* part of the ABCD model, and for your efforts to be successful you need to also consider the other parts of the model. For instance:

A: How does introducing the model align with your DEI strategy and vision? What will success look like? How will you evaluate it? How will it work alongside your other DEI initiatives? Who will own the implementation? How does it fit into your DEI governance structures? Do you have a RACI matrix that spells out who is responsible, accountable, consulted and informed? (See references for more information on RACI.)

B: How do the behaviours in the model align with your existing competency or team development models? How do you get the top team role modelling The Inclusive Team™ behaviours?

C: What is the organisation's culture currently like? Will aspects of the model be particularly challenging? Are there other organisation-wide initiatives that may compete and slow your progress, or that you can collaborate with to increase impact? How does the context influence the teams' ability to develop The Inclusive Team™ behaviours?

D: What have successful change initiatives looked like in your organisation? What change management approaches work well? Who are the key stakeholders and influencers you need to get on board? Are the behaviours in the model aligned with your reward and recognition processes – are you rewarding the right behaviours or creating potential conflict by rewarding non-inclusive behaviours?

It is very easy to get hyper focused when implementing an initiative and I would strongly encourage you to step back and integrate the ABCD model into your thinking and planning.

CHANGE MANAGEMENT

The Design element of the ABCD model talks about taking a change management approach to planning and implementing DEI. My observation is that this is often overlooked when planning DEI initiatives, therefore I wanted to call it out specifically.

We have all seen the stats on the success rate of major change initiatives. Apparently, seventy percent of all change programmes fail to achieve their goals. According to McKinsey this is largely due to employee resistance and a lack of management support. (Sounds familiar!) They do, however, also say that when employees are truly invested in change it is thirty percent more likely to stick.

The model below captures six principles I use when working with my clients. This book isn't intended to provide a masterclass in change management, but I think it is helpful to highlight its importance, and to share some of the things I have found have a positive effect on the outcome of organisation-wide DEI initiatives. There is additional reading in the references for those who want to explore this further.

Strong Sponsorship

Easy to say, not so easy to do. However, any organisation- or department-wide initiative that doesn't have strong, visible and active senior level sponsorship is likely to fail to reach its potential.

This is not just getting senior leaders on board; it is helping them understand what sponsorship actually means. Be clear with your expectations. It is an active role that requires visible participation in and support of the initiative – simply attaching their name to an email is not enough.

It is also vital that the senior leaders role model and reinforce the change. This may involve running a The Inclusive Team™ workshop for the leadership team to help them understand what you are trying to achieve, to help them to role model inclusive behaviours and to get them working together to create a more inclusive and high performing leadership team.

People often ask if it is possible to build an inclusive culture effectively if you don't have strong sponsorship from the top. The harsh truth is you can, but it will be really slow and hard work. You can make some changes, but it's likely to be a lengthy process, and you are likely to come up against pockets of strong resistance because it's clear that senior leaders are not really behind the initiative.

To return to the analogy of rowing that I shared at the beginning of this book, if a team is a single rowing boat, then organisational change is a bit like trying to get a whole flotilla of rowing boats going in the same direction at roughly the same time. You know some will be faster than others and some may get a little lost along the way, but if the vision is clear and the senior leaders are leading from the front, you are likely to get there. If the senior leaders are a bit unsure of the direction and are not really committing, it is likely to slow things down. If there is active resistance in the senior leadership, it is the equivalent of having boats rowing in the opposite direction, clashing oars and creating confusion.

Inclusive Design

Inclusive design means involving a broad range of perspectives in the development of an idea or plan. Originating in the tech world with a focus on creating accessible software and devices, it has a broader application in organisations. It is about not going to the usual suspects for their views, but deliberately involving people who are often overlooked or excluded (the term commonly used is 'extreme users').

When it comes to change initiatives, a common mistake is to keep the change team small in an effort to move quickly. However, this often means that the initiative stalls down the line when resistance is encountered or important elements have not been considered. I talk more about this and give an example in the Flexibility section of the Adaptability chapter.

Involving employees from across the organisation in the planning of a change initiative ensures that a broad range of voices are heard. Think about diversity in the broadest sense: including demographics, department, level, customers and roles. This typically makes the plan better and helps reduce the likelihood of resistance further down the line.

I like to think of it as slowing down to speed up. If you slow down at the beginning and involve more people, you can speed up down the line as there will be fewer bumps in the road.

Inclusive Communication

Inclusive communication is about recognising that communication is a two-way activity in the change process and that people like to receive communication in different ways. Communication is about speaking *and* listening. Too many organisations spend many hours crafting careful statements about the changes they are planning, but very few hours listening to employees' thoughts and feelings about the change.

Communications specialists recommend that there are five key things that need to be communicated about any organisational change.

The Need: What is the rationale for the change? Simon Sinek encourages us to 'start with why' – and effective communication is about connecting to the hearts and minds of employees. In the case of DEI, it is about compliance, the business benefits and the moral perspective.

The Solution: What is the change and why is it the best fit for the problem and organisation?

Logistics: The plan for the change. Who is leading it and what support will be provided?

Commitment: How important is it? What resources are being allocated to ensure it is successful?

Impact: How will this impact what they do? What are you asking them to do differently? Note that this may vary for different groups, therefore local leaders are often best placed to share this information.

Remember that large-scale corporate messages are not enough. It is important that messages are repeated in different ways, by different people, and that managers are equipped to have *'what's in it for me?'* conversations at a local level. In the context you work, what usual communication channels can you utilise? Do you need to take into account any special circumstances? The references include a blog post by communications specialists h&h which is a helpful summary of things to consider when thinking about internal communications.

As an example, a client of mine has a very dispersed workforce who don't have access to computers. They use team meetings and location noticeboards as key communication channels. They recently produced a fantastic video that shared their dedication to DEI to be shown during team meetings. As part of the design process, they conducted some focus groups with an early version of the new video and received some very helpful feedback, including a suggestion to provide subtitles in Polish because of the high number of Polish employees. They had not initially considered this, but because they took an inclusive design perspective they were able to create more inclusive communications.

Build Momentum

This is about gradually gaining buy-in, so the initiative gains momentum of its own and reaches a tipping point. I find Greg Satell's book *Cascades* very helpful in understanding how to create momentum for transformational change.

He suggests that transformation is created by 'small groups, loosely connected, and united by a common purpose'. This is based on the observation that we take social cues from those around us, such as friends, colleagues, neighbours and family members.

I particularly like Satell's framework as it aligns well with the concept of changing the organisation one inclusive team at a time – the teams who adopt The Inclusive Team™ model are the small groups connected by a common purpose of creating a more inclusive and high performing workplace.

I have summarised the core framework he uses below, and I recommend reading the book to get a deeper understanding.

Define: Create a clear sense of purpose by (i) identifying current concerns (ii) creating a future focused vision that is better than the current situation (iii) identifying a change that is the bridge between the current concerns and the vision (iv) identifying the core values that support your vision.

Plan: Create a clear plan by (i) stakeholder mapping to identify supporters and resistors (ii) identifying the pillars that support the status quo in your organisation and you therefore need to influence (e.g. unions, shareholders, politics, etc.) (iii) track support of stakeholders and pillars over time.

Incidentally, I prefer the title of *Analyse* rather than *Plan* for this phase! I think the next phase is more aligned with planning. You could use the onion diagram and Flexibility exercise in the Adaptability chapter to help with this phase.

Activate: Turn the plan into tangible actions (i) designing activities to mobilise the stakeholders and pillars you identified in the plan (or *analyse*) phase (ii) using the allies you have identified in your stakeholder map to influence the pillars (iii) planning how you will use a range of platforms (e.g. social media, internal communication channels) to align and connect groups around a common purpose.

Think about how you will connect the teams who are using The Inclusive Team™ model so they can share learning and create a visible movement that others will want to join.

Small pilot programmes in departments who like to be early adopters and lead the way, or with teams who are visible and have influence can be very effective in creating a FOMO (fear of missing out) effect.

I do not recommend starting with your most difficult and challenging people or teams. I've seen too many great initiatives dead in the water because the organisation thought that inviting their harshest critics to the pilot was a great way of stress testing the initiative. This high-risk strategy rarely pays off, in my experience. Piloting is a time for carefully testing things out and revising the approach. One vocal person who didn't enjoy themselves can have a huge negative impact on the desire of others to come on board with the initiative and can stop the train in its tracks. If you opened a new restaurant, you wouldn't want high profile food critics or the Michelin inspectors in on your first night!

Secure Resources

One of my main frustrations with the world of DEI is that people have been recruited into Head of DEI roles with no team, no positional power, a tiny budget, and then they are expected to change the world. If you are offered a role like this – do not take it. Go somewhere they take DEI seriously enough to invest money and resources.

The same applies to change initiatives in organisations. You need enough people and budget to make the change happen. This means people who have DEI as part of their job description/objectives – not just as an unrecognised and unpaid side hustle to their day-job.

It means involving people in the project who have the time and skills to ensure success. These may be change management professionals, internal communications experts or learning and development professionals. Don't try to do it all on your own. Be honest about what your skills are and what time you have available, then fill in the gaps with the time and expertise of others.

Ensure Alignment

This links to the ABCD model of systemic DEI that I covered earlier. You need to consider any DEI initiative in relation to the other parts of the model. When there is alignment, the impact of your activity is maximised.

It is important that your change doesn't happen in a vacuum and is aligned with other elements in the organisation – these may be strategies, other change initiatives, existing systems and processes or other training and development.

This topic is covered in depth with examples in the Alignment chapter, so jump back to it if you want a reminder.

RESISTANCE

We explored the challenge of resistance in Chapter Six, with a particular focus on the individual resistance we can experience in the moment during a workshop or when working at a team level.

When implementing change at a wider departmental or organisational level, the resistance may show itself in different ways and in different places throughout the system. However, when you are trying to create a more inclusive culture in your organisation, you can be confident that you will encounter opposition at some point.

The key is to anticipate that it will occur and plan in advance to do everything you can to reduce the resistance people may feel.

If you are someone who likes to dive into projects and take quick action, this may feel slow and frustrating, but if you want to avoid strong and vocal resistance further down the line, I recommend paying close attention to the Systemic DEI and Change Management activities given throughout this chapter. You have to slow down to speed up. Pay particular attention to the following:

- Know your organisational system. Which people and pillars (see the building momentum section above) are allies and resistors? How will you engage with them?
- Create a clear, attractive vision of the future, showing how a more diverse, equitable and inclusive culture will make things better for *all*.
- Practise inclusive design. Involve a broad range of people in creating your vision and plan.
- Ensure you have strong senior level sponsors, and they actively support your initiative.
- Build momentum by connecting pockets of supporters (teams who adopt The Inclusive Team™ approach).

EVALUATION, RETURN ON INVESTMENT AND NPS

Evaluation of any DEI initiative is essential. You need to know that what you are doing is making a difference, and how to adjust things if you are not getting the results you want. Key stakeholders may ask also you to provide evidence of impact.

I recommend you avoid trying to prove Return on Investment (ROI). Unless you can quantify all the expected outcomes from your initiative, have a lot of time and resources to carry out an evaluation, and can prove that the outcomes are solely as a result of that initiative, you are on a fool's errand. I recommend you focus on measuring impact and do not try to attach a monetary value to that impact.

Outlined below are three key topics to consider when evaluating an initiative. They apply equally whether you work with one team or with a whole organisation; it's just the methodology might be different. It is *absolutely essential* you consider these at the beginning of the project. It is really challenging to be asked later down the line to prove impact and work retrospectively to answer these questions. Believe me, I have been there!

If the implementation team work through these questions, together they will be able to start to build a comprehensive evaluation methodology and plan.

Note that if you are working with an external provider, do not try to completely outsource evaluation to them. They will not have access to all the information needed to evaluate properly, and you need to make sure that you agree what is to be measured and why. It should be a collaborative effort between the internal team and the external provider.

Vision and Outcomes

What specifically are you trying to achieve with this initiative? You would be surprised how many organisations I have come across who haven't clearly articulated the expected outcome of the initiative.

How will you know when you get there? What will be different? How will you measure the difference? What expectations do your different stakeholders have? What are your Key Performance Indicators (KPIs)? I recommend you identify both quantitative and qualitative methods of data collection.

Baseline

Where are you now, and where do you want to be? Do you have baseline measures? This is crucial: you need to know where you are today as well as where you want to get to in the future. You may find that some baseline data you need is missing and you need to collect it at the beginning of the project.

Achievability

Is what you are expecting a realistic expectation given your budget, culture, and other competing factors? Have you identified any opposing forces that may impact your ability to be successful? What other initiatives are taking place that may also influence the outcomes (in a positive or negative way)?

KIRKPATRICK

Many organisations use the Kirkpatrick Model (see below) as a framework, and some may see it as old news. I have reviewed various other evaluation models, but I believe that Kirkpatrick is as good as any as long as you use it properly.

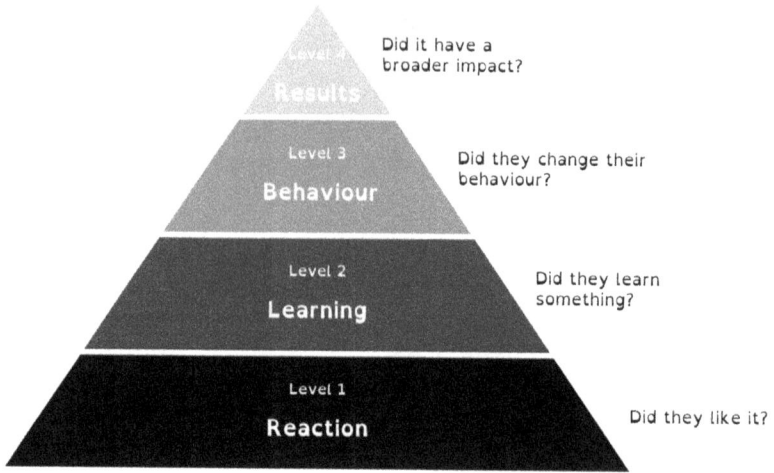

I find that it is very common for organisations to never get past evaluating at level two. The further up the levels you go and the more time and effort you are willing to invest in gathering data the better your evaluation will be.

Levels one and two

Levels one and two can be measured at the time of an intervention through an evaluation form filled out during it or immediately afterwards. It is commonly known as the 'happy sheet'! It is simple, quick and cheap. It is also not a good measure of whether an initiative has impact, because an individual's enjoyment of something is not necessarily correlated with whether they will change their behaviour.

In fact, I would argue that often it is the opposite. A coaching client of mine was recently asked by her line manager if she had enjoyed the work we had been doing together. She and I both laughed, because she had found many of the sessions tough. We had been digging into things that she found difficult and challenging. She didn't particularly enjoy them. I told the line manager that a better question was to ask if she found the coaching sessions helpful, which she indicated that she had.

Think about the most impactful learning you have had in your career. Was it when you were loving life and enjoying yourself, or when you were outside of your comfort zone? I have asked this question to hundreds of leaders, and the vast majority report that their most important learning came when they were challenged and stretched.

This highlights the danger of relying too heavily on level one and two evaluations. So many organisations seem to be obsessed with evaluating their development initiatives and training using the Net Promoter Score (NPS), which is a score out of ten that indicates how likely you would be to recommend the course to someone else. I have seen great programmes cancelled because of NPS scores below an organisation's arbitrary cut off point.

If you ask the NPS question at or immediately after a participant has attended a workshop, you typically get a measure of whether they enjoyed themselves. A much better way would be to ask them the same question after they have had time to reflect on and apply the content to their real world – as part of a level three evaluation.

Level three

The challenge with level three is that you need to give people time to apply the learning before you can evaluate whether their behaviour has changed. The level of response you get – and therefore the validity of your data – will largely depend on how much time and effort you are willing to invest in collecting feedback.

On a basic level you can send an online survey to participants. You will need to chase (and maybe even incentivise) them to respond. Individual phone interviews tend to get a better response and allow you to dig deeper and get examples. However, you are still only getting the perspective of the individual.

Feedback from their manager and/or colleagues will give you a more rounded perspective and can be particularly powerful if you have used a 360 survey before the programme as a baseline.

As an initiative using The Inclusive Team™ model is aimed at team level behaviours, you could repeat the ten-question survey at regular intervals to view the progress the team is making.

Level four

I have rarely seen organisations trying to evaluate level four impact. This is because it is really difficult. It goes back to the initial questions I posed about expected impact and how that impact is to be measured. Level four evaluation requires identification of organisation-level measures that the initiative is expected to influence.

For example, if the expected impact is an increase in inclusive behaviours across the organisation, there may be Diversity and Inclusion questions in the organisation's employee survey with the expectation that the initiative will result in an improvement in the scores. Or if the organisation links DEI to innovation, there may be an expected increase in new product ideas. Or perhaps the impact is predicted to be an increase in the recruitment of under-represented groups into the organisation. All of these things can be measured, but you need a pre-initiative baseline measure.

The challenge is that when you are looking at broader impact, it is very difficult to tie outcomes to the specific initiative, as it is unlikely that the initiative will be the only thing going on in the organisation that influences how inclusively individuals behave. Indeed, it shouldn't be the only thing happening in the organisation, as the most successful change initiatives will combine a number of complementary activities targeting the same change in behaviours.

To get round this, I have used more qualitative methods (surveys with open ended questions and phone interviews) to get examples from participants that they link to taking part in the specific initiative you are trying to evaluate. This isn't perfect, and I have found that individuals find it fairly easy to identify behaviour change (level 3) but much more difficult to identify organisational impact (level 4).

The important thing is to be clear at the outset what your expected outcomes are, and what method you are going to use to measure it. Sometimes you may have to do some work at the beginning to create a baseline data because it is not something you are currently measuring.

I realise this might all seem a little doom and gloom and a lot of hard work. I don't want to put you off evaluating your The Inclusive Team™ implementation. I just want to encourage you to think carefully about it at the beginning of the project, and to create realistic and measurable objectives and a methodology that means you are able to invest time and effort collecting useful data.

An Alternative Perspective on Evaluation

Most evaluation methodologies I have seen place an emphasis on the participants evaluating the initiative. This invites them to see themselves as passive recipients of the activity – something is being done to them. We ask them, 'How good do you think this initiative was?' or 'How well did we do?' It encourages them to critique the initiative rather than ask themselves, 'How do I make the most of this opportunity being given to me?'

It does not recognise that the outcome of any initiative is also down to the investment and effort of each individual. We do not ask them how much work they put in. We do not ask them to reflect on what they could have done differently to ensure the initiative was a success. We do not ask them to reflect on what they learnt about themselves when they didn't enjoy an activity. Our questions do not encourage them to take responsibility for their own learning and behaviour.

As the philosophy of The Inclusive Team™ is to create a shared sense of responsibility for creating an inclusive culture, how about we put a different spin on our evaluation? The questions we ask encourage the participants to see themselves as active players in the success of the initiative.

I have designed an alternative workshop evaluation survey available to download with the other materials that accompany this book. Why not try it out and experiment with a different approach to evaluation?

References

10 principles of leading change management (DeAnne Aguirre and Micah Alpern, 2014) - https://www.strategy-business.com/article/00255

Start with Why (Simon Sinek, 2011) - https://amzn.to/3G7LPDG

Could A RACI Chart Boost Your Productivity? (Dana Miranda, Rob Watts) - https://www.forbes.com/uk/advisor/business/software/raci-chart/

Ensure your talent system is built with an inclusive design - Korn Ferry - https://www.kornferry.com/insights/featured-topics/diversity-equity-inclusion/talent-system-is-built-with-inclusive-design

Cascades – How to create a movement that drives transformational change (Greg Satell, 2019) - https://amzn.to/3MSspXc

How to effectively plan an internal communications campaign - h&h blog - https://handhcomms.co.uk/effectively-plan-internal-comms-campaigns/

ACKNOWLEDGEMENTS

A huge thank you to the team at Authors and Co who have supported me and helped make this book a beautiful thing that I am proud to have written.

Thanks also to my good friends Jenny Kidby, Claire Kelly and Emma Klapsia who read my early ramblings and gave excellent feedback and advice.

And I would like to acknowledge the many authors and researchers whose books, articles and papers I read whilst researching this book. I truly feel like I am standing on the shoulders of giants.

And finally, thank you to the many colleagues and clients I have worked with over the years. This book would be a few pages long if it wasn't for you!

About the Author

Melody is the founder of Liberare Consulting, a DE&I, Leadership and coaching consultancy. She is also the host of 'The Secret Resume' Podcast.

She is a Business Psychologist with over twenty years consulting experience, and before establishing her own company was a Senior Client Partner and UK DEI practice lead for a large global consultancy.

Melody has worked with clients across a wide range of sectors and geographies and specialises in DEI, team development, executive coaching and leadership development.

She is obsessed with people and what makes them tick. To support this, she is in the final year of training to be a Practitioner in Developmental Trauma Therapy.

Melody lives with her daughter Holly and dog Lyra. She enjoys gardening and making things to clutter up her home at a weekly ceramics class.

in linkedin.com/in/melody-moore-liberare

Resources

You can download the exercises and handouts accompanying this book via a private section of the Liberare Consulting website, available only to those who have purchased *The Inclusive Team* book.

Use this link or the QR code to register and get the password:

https://liberareconsulting.co.uk/the-inclusive-team-download-registration/

RESOURCES

You can find more information about The Inclusive Team™ online training and diagnostic here:

https://liberareconsulting.co.uk/the-inclusive-team-programme

If you want to know more about Liberare Consulting you can find us here:

https://liberareconsulting.co.uk